ARE YOU "NORMAL"? 2

BY MARK SHULMAN

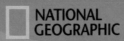

NATIONAL GEOGRAPHIC

WASHINGTON, D.C.

Published by the National Geographic Society

John M. Fahey, *Chairman.of the Board and Chief Executive Officer*

Declan Moore, *Executive Vice President; President, Publishing and Travel*

Melina Gerosa Bellows, *Executive Vice President; Chief Creative Officer, Books, Kids, and Family*

Prepared by the Book Division

Hector Sierra, *Senior Vice President and General Manager*

Nancy Laties Feresten, *Senior Vice President, Kids Publishing and Media*

Jay Sumner, *Director of Photography, Children's Publishing*

Jennifer Emmett, *Vice President, Editorial Director, Children's Books*

Eva Absher-Schantz, *Design Director, Kids Publishing and Media*

R. Gary Colbert, *Production Director*

Jennifer A. Thornton, *Director of Managing Editorial*

Staff for This Book

Becky Baines, *Project Editor*

Kathryn Robbins, *Art Director*

Lori Epstein, *Senior Photo Editor*

Ariane Szu-Tu, *Editorial Assistant*

Callie Broaddus, *Design Production Assistant*

Hillary Moloney, *Associate Photo Editor*

Grace Hill, *Associate Managing Editor*

Joan Gossett, *Production Editor*

Lewis R. Bassford, *Production Manager*

Susan Borke, *Legal and Business Affairs*

Anne McCormack, *Director of Digital Media*

Sara Zeglin, *Digital Producer*

Production Services

Phillip L. Schlosser, *Senior Vice President*

Chris Brown, *Vice President, NG Book Manufacturing*

George Bounelis, *Vice President, Production Services*

Nicole Elliott, *Manager*

Rachel Faulise, *Manager*

Robert L. Barr, *Manager*

CELEBRATING
◀125▶
YEARS

The National Geographic Society is one of the world's largest nonprofit scientific and educational organizations. Founded in 1888 to "increase and diffuse geographic knowledge," the Society's mission is to inspire people to care about the planet. It reaches more than 400 million people worldwide each month through its official journal, *National Geographic*, and other magazines; National Geographic Channel; television documentaries; music; radio; films; books; DVDs; maps; exhibitions; live events; school publishing programs; interactive media; and merchandise. National Geographic has funded more than 10,000 scientific research, conservation and exploration projects and supports an education program promoting geographic literacy. For more information, visit nationalgeographic.com.

For more information, please call 1-800-NGS LINE (647-5463) or write to the following address:
National Geographic Society
1145 17th Street N.W.
Washington, DC 20036-4688 U.S.A.

Visit us online at
www.nationalgeographic.com/books

For librarians and teachers:
www.ngchildrensbooks.org

More for kids from National Geographic:
kids.nationalgeographic.com

For information about special discounts for bulk purchases, please contact National Geographic Books Special Sales:
ngspecsales@ngs.org

For rights or permissions inquiries, please contact National Geographic Books Subsidiary Rights: ngbookrights@ngs.org

Printed in Hong Kong
13/THK/1

CON-TENTS

ARE YOU "NORMAL"? 2

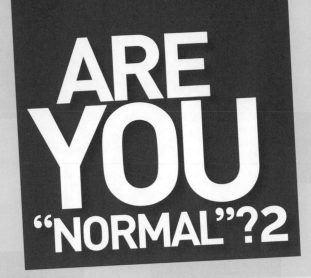

ARE YOU "NORMAL"?2

WHAT'S SO NORMAL ABOUT NORMAL?

FOR SOME REASON, WE ALL WANT TO KNOW IF WE'RE NORMAL.

Which are you? The person who thinks you aren't normal and you want to be? Or the person who thinks you're too normal, and you want to stand out a little more? Either way, this book is for you. Are you a picky eater . . . or do you pick strange foods? Do you have sleepovers with 30 friends . . . or just with your stuffed animals? Would you rather travel by foot . . . by car . . . by helicopter . . . or by water mammal?

THE ANSWER IS . . .

You're normal. And the other answer is . . . nobody's normal. There's no such thing. What's normal for your age isn't normal for Grandma. What's normal on a trampoline isn't normal in a rowboat. And what's normal at your dinner table is downright weird around the world.

HOW CAN WE TELL?

The busy, brainy folks at National Geographic surveyed thousands of school-age kids to learn the ins and outs of their likes and dislikes. The online response was tremendous. (Remember that time the Internet stopped working for a while? That was our fault!) We juggled the figures and crunched the numbers. Best of all, those colorful, fun, and informative replies became this colorful, fun, and informative book. Remember, your answers reflect your own tastes and opinions. And every person has different tastes and opinions. What would it be like if you had the same opinion as everyone else?

VERY STRANGE.

Kids and their lives are like thumbprints and snowflakes. No two are alike. So if you bring your pet to school, that's weird. Unless your kid brother is your pet. Then, not so weird. You see how it works?

YOU'RE SO WEIRD, YOU'RE NORMAL!

ABOUT THE NUMBERS

HOW DO I USE THE BOOK?

1 READ THE QUESTIONS.

2 ANSWER THE QUESTIONS.

3 TOTAL UP YOUR WEIRD-O-METER POINTS FOR EACH CHAPTER.

4 LOWER NUMBERS = NORMAL
HIGHER NUMBERS = NOT SO NORMAL

5 GET DIFFERENT RESULTS FOR EACH CHAPTER.

6 IT'S COMPLETELY NORMAL TO HAVE FUN!

WHAT DO THESE NUMBERS MEAN?

Your answer to each question will be assigned Weird-O-Meter points located at the bottom of each page. Keep track of your score as you go through the chapter, so you can determine your overall Weird-O-Meter ranking for each section. The numbers range from 1 to 4, so even if your answer is totally out there, and only 2 out of 100 kids answered the same way, the highest you can get is 4 points. That way, one super-strange (or super-normal) answer won't totally throw off your number.

WHERE DO I FIND OUT HOW NORMAL I AM?

At the end of each chapter, you'll total up your points to see how normal (or weird) you are compared with all the other kids.

You might find you're totally weird in one category and totally normal in another. Or you might be about the same from category to category but vary a lot from question to question. Any way you score is totally your own and totally fine.

(MORE)
ABOUT THE
NUMBERS

WHEN WILL THESE NUMBERS MAKE SENSE?

You may not have learned fractions or percentages yet. But don't worry, it's not so hard. Imagine 10 kids in a row. If 5 of them agree on the same answer, then that's the same as writing "half the kids agree" or "5 out of 10 agree" or "1/2 agree" or "50% agree."

A PERCENT EQUALS 1 PART OF 100.

So, 50 parts of 100 = 50 percent = 50% = 50/100 = 1/2 = 50 people out of every 100. The lower the percent, the less normal something is. If 97% of your friends wear pants on their legs, it's super normal. If 3% wear them on their heads, it's really, really NOT normal.

really normal 97%   3% really not normal

So, if 10,000 kids answer a question, and 5,000 kids answer the same way, then that's the same as half, or 1/2, or 50%, or . . . you get the idea.

HERE'S A CHART. SEE IF YOU CAN SPOT THE PATTERNS.

HOW MANY KIDS ANSWERED THE SAME WAY?	AS WORDS	AS A PERCENT
Half 1/2	5 out of 10	50%
A third 1/3	About 3 out of 10 or 1 out of 3	About 33%
A fourth or a quarter 1/4	1 out of 4	25%
A fifth 1/5	2 out of 10 or 1 out of 5	20%
A sixth 1/6	1 out of 6	About 17%
A seventh 1/7	1 out of 7	About 14%
An eighth 1/8	1 out of 8	About 12%
A ninth 1/9	1 out of 9	About 11%
A tenth 1/10	1 out of 10	10%

Like all polls, these results represent the opinions of the people surveyed. The people who answer are called a sample. If a sample is big enough and similar enough to the population in general, then it can show the breakdown of what the larger population thinks at a particular time. If a sample is not large enough, or not assembled scientifically, then it is not always a good indicator of everyone's opinion. People can also answer questions differently depending on how the questions are asked. These different factors can lead to different results. So polls are useful tools for finding out what people think, but they are not perfect. Try asking your friends or family or class these questions and you'll see that your poll gets slightly different results.

You might notice that if you add up the percentages in each answer, some are slightly above or below 100%. That's because in some cases the original data was rounded up or down. The results will still give you an idea of the bigger picture. The data collected for this book is up to date as of May 2013.

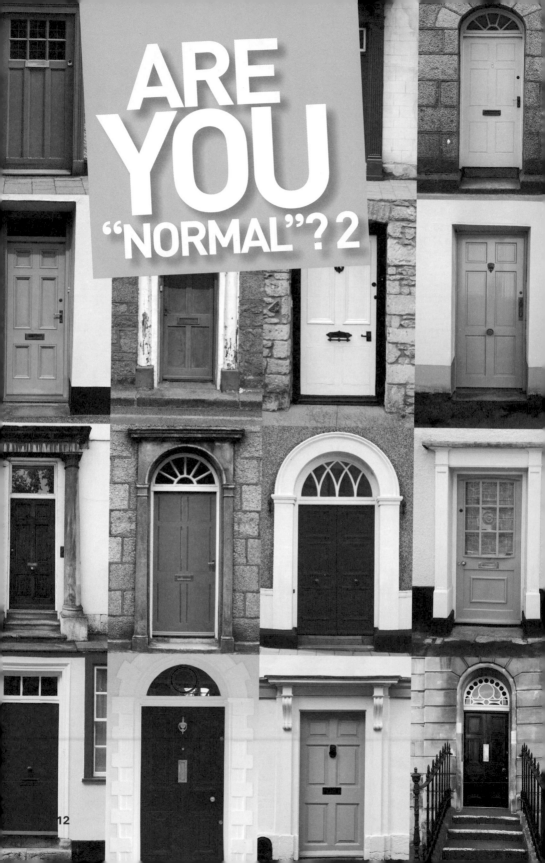

ARE YOU "NORMAL"? 2

12

HOME

HOME QUIZ

BE SURE TO KEEP TRACK OF YOUR ANSWERS!

1 WHICH FLOOR DO YOU SLEEP ON?
- Basement
- First floor
- Second floor
- Third floor
- Fourth floor or higher

2 DO YOU LIVE WITH A KID WHO ISN'T YOUR BROTHER OR SISTER?
- No
- Yes

3 HAVE YOU EVER BEEN GROUNDED?
- Not yet!
- Yes, for a day or less
- Yes, for up to a week
- Yes, for up to a month
- Yes, for more than a month

4 HOW CLOSE IS YOUR NEAREST GROCERY STORE?
- Walking distance
- Biking distance
- Driving distance
- I live in the same building.

5 ARE YOU EXPECTED TO SAVE TOWARD YOUR COLLEGE EDUCATION?

- Yes
- No
- Not yet, but I can see it coming.

6 DO YOU CLEAN UP AFTER YOURSELF?

- Usually
- Sometimes
- Are you kidding? I'm a kid!

7 DO YOU HAVE A NEIGHBOR WHO'S GOT THE BEST SNACKS?

- No one in my neighborhood has good snacks.
- No, they're all good.
- Yes, a friend's
- Yes, mine

8 WHERE IN THE HOUSE DO YOU SPEND MOST OF YOUR COMPUTER TIME?

- Bedroom
- Office
- Family room
- Basement
- Attic
- Living room
- Kitchen
- Other
- I don't have a computer at home.

9 HOW MANY PEOPLE LIVE IN YOUR HOME (BESIDES YOU)?

- 1
- 2
- 3
- 4
- 5
- 6
- 7
- 8
- 9
- 10
- More than 10

15

1

Z^Z ^Z ^Z

SNORE
ON THE
FLOOR?

Which floor do you sleep on? No, no, not on the floor. We mean, on which floor of your home is your bed?

- ◖ **Second is first:** 42% head up a flight before laying down for the night.

- ◖ **First is second:** Another 40% don't go up to bed—they go across.

- ◔ **Third is third:** At bedtime, 8% go up, up, and away.

- ◔ **Minus-one is fourth:** 5% of kids sleep sound underground in the basement.

- ◔ **Fourth (and up) is fifth:** To the fourth floor and beyond is where 5% ride the elevator to bed.

WEIRD-**O**-METER FIRST/SECOND = 2,
ALL OTHER ANSWERS = 4

2 AT HOME WITH YOUR HOMEYS?

Do you live with a kid who isn't your brother or sister?

91% MOSTLY, NO. Nine out of 10 kids say it's all relative at home.

SOME SAY YES. Nearly 1 in 10 kids have a built-in sleepover every night of the week. **9%**

WEIRD-O-METER   NO = 1, YES = 4

3

EVER BEEN GROUNDED?

Do the crime and do the time.
Half the kids have been sentenced
to hang out with their stuff.

For up to a day? About 1 in 5 kids
(21%) served short time.

For up to a week? About 1 in 5 different kids (19%) didn't see daylight for
days.

For up to a month? 1 in 20 (5%) had
weeks and weeks to think about
never doing that thing again.

For more than a month? Wow.
Another 1 in 20 (5%) did more than
30 days.

The other half (50%) just don't
understand. That is, until they
do that thing . . .

WEIRD-O-METER   UP TO A DAY = 2, UP TO A WEEK = 3, UP TO A
MONTH OR MORE = 4, NEVER BEEN GROUNDED = 2

4 IN CASE OF BLIZZARD...

How close is the nearest grocery store?

- Driving distance is the norm.
  40% NEED A CAR.

- The grocer is closer for some.
  35% CAN WALK.

- Others can two-wheel it.
  23% PEDAL.

- **2% CAN HOP TO THE SHOP IN THEIR SLIPPERS.**
  Now that's what you call a convenience store!

WEIRD-O-METER DRIVE/WALK = 2, BIKE = 3, IN THE BUILDING = 4

5

DOLLAR$ FOR DIPLOMA$

ARE YOU EXPECTED TO SAVE TOWARD YOUR COLLEGE EDUCATION?

About 4 in 10 kids (38%) SAY YES, saving for school is in the budget.

More than 2 in 10 kids (23%) SAY NO, they don't have to collect cash for college.

And the other 4 in 10 kids (39%) SAY THEY HAVEN'T BEEN ASKED TO SAVE—YET. But their parents will probably make them pay some day.

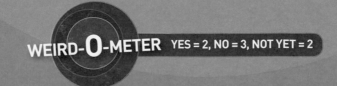

WEIRD-O-METER   YES = 2, NO = 3, NOT YET = 2

6 ARE YOU NEAT?

C'MON, HONESTLY . . .
DO YOU CLEAN UP AFTER YOURSELF?

45%
I'm usually a HUMAN VACUUM cleaner.

35%
I'm sometimes CLEAN and sometimes CLUTTERED.

20%
I make any area a DISASTER AREA.

WEIRD-O-METER USUALLY = 2, SOMETIMES = 2, NEVER = 3

7 WHAT'S GOOD IN THE HOOD?

Do you have a neighbor who's got the best snacks?

"The food's all good, all around the block," say 1 in 4 kids (25%).

"My friends have fantastic food," say about 1 in 5 kids (19%).

"My home is home-base for the hungry," say nearly 1 in 5 kids (18%).

And the other 1 in 3 kids (37%) say there's nothing good in their neighborhood, their zip code, maybe even their entire state.

WEIRD-O-METER EVERYONE HAS GOOD SNACKS = 2, A FRIEND'S HOUSE = 3, MY HOUSE = 3, NO HOUSE HAS GOOD SNACKS = 2

8 WHICH ROOM HAS THE WINDOWS— OR THE MAC?

Where in the house do you spend most of your computer time?

- 25% [browse] in the bedroom.
- 24% [log in] in the living room.
- 14% [organize online] in the office.
- 12% [friend friends] in the family room.
- 6% [kill time] in the kitchen.
- 3% [boot up] in the basement.
- 1% [access apps] in the attic.
- 2% [delete] and don't have a computer at home.
- 13% [surf] somewhere else.

WEIRD-O-METER BEDROOM/LIVING ROOM/OFFICE/FAMILY ROOM = 2, KITCHEN = 3, BASEMENT/ATTIC/ NO COMPUTER = 4, SOMEPLACE ELSE = 2

9 HOW MANY'S A HOUSEFUL?

How many people live in your home (besides you)?

Remember, guinea pigs and goldfish don't count.

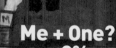

Me + One?
= 3%

Me + Two?
= 13%

Me + Three?
= 32%

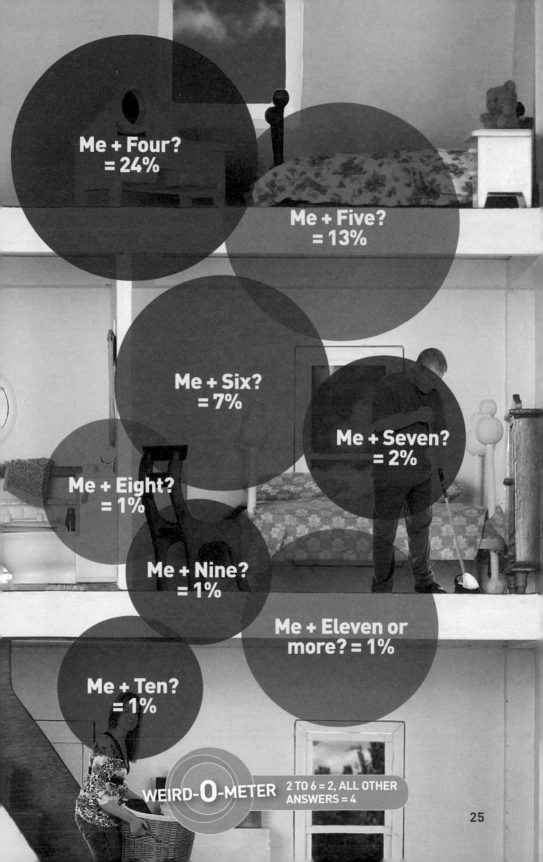

Me + Four?
= 24%

Me + Five?
= 13%

Me + Six?
= 7%

Me + Seven?
= 2%

Me + Eight?
= 1%

Me + Nine?
= 1%

Me + Eleven or
more? = 1%

Me + Ten?
= 1%

WEIRD-O-METER 2 TO 6 = 2, ALL OTHER
ANSWERS = 4

25

WHERE ARE YOU ON THE WEIRD-O-METER?

ADD UP YOUR SCORE AND YOU'LL GET A WEIRDNESS NUMBER YOU CAN WRITE **HOME** ABOUT.

YOU'RE AS NORMAL AS SLEEPING ON A BED.

For you, home is where the heart is. And yours doesn't even have that many people in it. (The home, we mean, not the heart.) Got doors? Windows? Normal. A floor? Super normal. And you usually clean up that floor. Your home may not be the most fascinating or entertaining place on Earth, but it's almost certainly got walls, with electrical outlets for plugging in fascinating and entertaining things.

22–27

YOU'RE AS NORMAL AS SLEEPING ON A HAMMOCK.

Got something different going on in the house? Maybe you've got the best snacks in the hood—which is good—because you're also probably likely to get grounded for a month. Home's fine, and you sure spend time in it, but you're just as likely to go out and about, especially if you can travel to stores without a ride. For you, there's no place like home, but it's good to have some nice backup places, too.

28–33

YOU'RE AS NORMAL AS SLEEPING ON A BEARSKIN. WITH A LIVE BEAR IN IT.

Even if you do have a bed, you probably have 12 cousins and a Saint Bernard sleeping alongside you. You're as normal as using the computer in the garden shed and eating all your meals out there, too. And is that your bed in the shed? That'll be good for the Saint Bernard, but for those cousins? Probably not so much. You may not be anything close to normal, which is why your nearest grocery store is either an hour away—or in your building.

ARE YOU
YOU
"NORMAL"? 2

SCHOOL

SCHOOL QUIZ

BE SURE TO KEEP TRACK OF YOUR ANSWERS!

1 **AT YOUR LAST SCHOOL BOOK FAIR, WHAT DID YOU END UP GETTING?**

- Chapter book
- Silly or weird book
- Graphic novel
- Science book
- History book
- Picture book
- Puzzle or game book
- Poetry book
- Something that wasn't even a book
- Nothing

2 **DID YOUR SCHOOL CLOSE IN THE LAST YEAR BECAUSE OF WEATHER?**

- No days—rats!
- A few days
- One day
- A lot of days

3 **HAVE YOU EVER PASSED A NOTE IN CLASS?**

- No
- Once
- A few times
- So many times, I should write a newspaper

4 **HOW DO YOU SIZE UP IN YOUR CLASS?**

- I'm the shortest.
- I'm on the shorter side.
- I'm middle of the pack.
- I'm among the tall.
- I'm the tallest.

5 HOW DO YOU USUALLY GET YOUR LUNCH ON SCHOOL DAYS?

- I usually bring it.
- I usually buy it.
- I do a mix of both.
- I eat lunch at home.

6 HOW'S THE FOOD AT YOUR SCHOOL?

- Yum!
- It's hit or miss . . .
- Yuck!
- Don't know. Never tried it.

7 WHAT NAME ARE YOU SUPPOSED TO USE FOR YOUR TEACHERS?

- Their last name
- Their first name
- Different rules for different teachers
- It's up to me.

8 WHO HELPS YOU WHEN THE HOMEWORK'S DUE?

- A parent
- A friend
- A teacher
- A sister
- A brother
- Another relative
- A tutor

1

WAS THE BOOK FAIR FAIR FOR YOU?

FOR A FEW MAGICAL DAYS OF THE YEAR, YOUR SCHOOL MORPHS INTO A GREAT BOOKSTORE.

So? What did you end up getting?

- **40% Chapter book**
- **9% Silly or weird book**
- **6% Graphic novel**
- **6% Science book**
- **3% History book**
- **3% Picture book**
- **3% Puzzle or game book**
- **1% Poetry book**
- **12% Something that wasn't even a book**
- **17% Nothing, not even a little eraser**

WEIRD-O-METER CHAPTER BOOK = 2, SILLY BOOK/GRAPHIC NOVEL/ SCIENCE BOOK/SOMETHING THAT WASN'T A BOOK/NOTHING = 3, ALL OTHER ANSWERS = 4

2 WEATHER? OR NOT?

Did your school close in the last year because of weather?

Almost 3 in 10 kids got a few days off.

Almost 1 in 7 kids had just one rotten day off for rotten weather.

1 in 9 kids said, "Yeah! Lots of days! It's all fun and . . . um . . . shoveling?"

A bit less than half got no days for snow days. But the weather was nice.

WEIRD-O-METER A FEW DAYS = 2, ONE DAY = 3, LOTS OF DAYS = 4, NO DAYS = 2

3 EVER PASSED A NOTE IN CLASS?

➤ ONCE?
1 in 8 kids gave it a try, then gave it a pass.

➤ A FEW TIMES?
More than 1 in 3 kids have scribbled on a few scraps.

➤ LOTS OF TIMES?
1 in 5 kids run their own printing press on school property.

➤ NEVER?
1 in 3 kids say those little scraps of paper are only for writing down homework assignments.

WEIRD-O-METER ONCE = 4, A FEW TIMES = 2, LOTS = 3, NEVER = 2

4 HIGH! HOW ARE YOU?

HOW DO YOU SIZE UP IN YOUR CLASS?

(9%) THE TALLEST—I TOWER OVER THE TEACHER.

(33%) TALLER THAN MOST—I'M A LARGE.

(30%) MEASURE ME A MEDIUM.

(20%) SHORTER THAN MOST—I'M ON THE SHORT LIST.

(8%) HERE'S THE LOWDOWN: I'M THE LOWEST DOWN.

WEIRD-O-METER TALLEST = 4, TALL/MEDIUM /SHORT = 2, SHORTEST = 4

5 WHAT'S YOUR LUNCH SOURCE?

How do you usually get your lunch on school days?

- **(44%) Bag, box, or barrel**—Nearly half of all kids lug their lunch. Maybe because they know what's in the hot lunches.

- **(25%) Platter, plate, or tray**—1 in 4 kids pick it up ready-made. Maybe because they know what's in the bags from home.

- **(20%) Here and there**—1 in 5 kids mix and match, hot and cold, sometimes bring, sometimes buy their lunches.

- **(11%) There's no plate like home**—1 in 9 kids do lunch where they do breakfast and dinner—at the family table. It's the best way to get seconds!

WEIRD-O-METER BRING = 2, BUY = 2, MIX IT UP = 3, EAT AT HOME = 4

6 EAT SCHOOL LUNCH? HOW'S THE FOOD?

GOOD, BAD, NEUTRAL, or never—whatever your opinion of your school's menu, you're pretty much normal.

➥ **28% Yum!**

➥ **25% It's hit or miss . . .**

➥ **27% Yuck!**

➥ **20% It's a mystery. Not the meat (maybe) but the meal (definitely). That's because I've never tried school lunches.**

WEIRD-O-METER YUM = 2, IT VARIES = 2, YUCK = 2, NEVER TRIED IT = 3

7 HELLO, YOUR NAME IS ...?

What name are you supposed to use for your teachers?

LAST NAMES GO FIRST: 2 in 3 kids call their teacher Mr. ___. Unless he's a woman. Then it's Ms. ___.

SAVE THE FIRST NAMES FOR FRIENDS: Only 1 in 12 kids call their teacher Ed or Erica.

GOTTA KEEP IT STRAIGHT: More than 1 in 6 kids have different name rules for different classrooms.

KIDS CALL THEM NAMES: Hopefully nice ones. 1 in 12 say the teachers don't care what they're called.

WEIRD-O-METER LAST NAME = 1, FIRST NAME = 4, DEPENDS ON THE TEACHER = 3, IT'S UP TO ME = 4

8 HAVE A HOMEWORK HELPER?

WHO HELPS YOU WHEN THE HOMEWORK'S DUE?

- **67% A parent pitches in.**
- 11% My friend is a friend indeed.
- 9% I learn from my teacher.
- 5% My sister shares her smarts.
- 3% My brother brings his brains.
- 3% Another relative helps me make the grade.
- 2% A tutor helps me toot my own horn.

WEIRD-O-METER PARENT = 1, FRIEND/TEACHER = 3, ALL OTHER ANSWERS = 4

WHERE ARE YOU ON THE WEIRD-O-METER?

ADD UP YOUR SCORE AND YOU'LL **LEARN** A LOT ABOUT YOURSELF.

1–19

YOU'RE AS NORMAL AS GOING TO SCHOOL ON MONDAY.

For you, school's cool—at least most of the time. Your teacher (whose first name is either Mr. or Ms.) thinks you're totally average (in height) and you eat an average lunch (probably out of a brown bag). And though you sometimes pass notes, you pay attention to the teacher even more often. At your last school book fair, we bet you got a book *and* an eraser.

YOU'RE AS NORMAL AS GOING TO SCHOOL ON SATURDAY.

What's your favorite part of school? Your friends? The lessons? The fossilized gum under the tables? Chances are you like lunchtime, even the mysterious meals they make for you. If you eat at school, that is. You very likely call your teachers by their first name and yourself by your last name. At your last book fair, it's possible you brought home an encyclopedia. Maybe even all 26 volumes!

YOU'RE AS NORMAL AS GOING TO SCHOOL ON THANKSGIVING.

So you ended up here, huh? Why's that? 30 snow days? Or was it a volcano? You could be 12 inches tall, or 12 feet. And you probably pass more notes than a concert pianist. Congratulations! You certainly make the grade as far as standing out. At your last school book fair, you probably took home all the books on the table. And the table. And the signs. And the vice principal.

ARE
YOU
"NORMAL"? 2

FRIENDS

FRIENDS QUIZ

BE SURE TO KEEP TRACK OF YOUR ANSWERS!

1 DO YOU HAVE ONE VERY BEST FRIEND?
- Yes
- No
- I've got more than one very best friend.

2 HAVE YOU AND YOUR FRIENDS EVER CREATED A SECRET LANGUAGE?
- No
- Yes

3 HOW DOES YOUR ALLOWANCE COMPARE TO YOUR FRIENDS'?
- I get less than most of them.
- I get about the same.
- I get more than all of them.
- I don't know.

4 DO YOU HAVE ANY FRIENDS WHO ARE TWINS?
- Yes, and I hang out with only one of them.
- Yes, and I hang out with both of them.
- No

5
HOW OLD WERE YOU WHEN YOU HAD YOUR FIRST OFFICIAL SLEEPOVER?

- Under 6
- 6
- 7
- 8
- 9
- 10
- 11
- 12
- Over 12
- Haven't had one yet

6
HOW DID YOUR FIRST "AWAY" SLEEPOVER END?

- Stayed the whole night
- Went home in the middle of the night
- Went home before bedtime
- Haven't had one yet

7
WHAT DO YOU DO IF SOMEONE IS RUDE TO YOU?

- I ignore the person.
- I'm rude back.
- I'm nice back.
- It depends on HOW rude.

8
WHAT DO YOU DO IF YOU'VE FORGOTTEN SOMEONE'S NAME?

- Ask again
- Try something clever to find out
- Ask someone else secretly
- Fake it and hope you find out later

45

BEST
OF THE
BEST
OF THE
BEST?

Do you have ONE very best friend?

More than 1 in 3 (37%) said, "I've got a great best friend."

More than half (53%) said, "I've got more than one best friend."

And 1 in 10 (10%) said, "Not now, not yet, or just not happening" on the best-friend front.

WEIRD-O-METER   YES = 2, MORE THAN ONE = 2, NO = 4

2 GLORK ZINK POO-DOO?

Ever created a secret language with your friends?

47%
Miffle fleej zagwonk vlup queeeeez.

53%
And the other half said they haven't.

WEIRD-O-METER   YES = 3, NO = 2

47

3 WHO'S REALLY CA$HING IN?

HOW DOES YOUR ALLOWANCE COMPARE TO YOUR FRIENDS'?

◑ Dearest Grandmother always said, "It's simply not polite to talk about money." Smile, Grandma. Exactly half (50%) of kids say they've got NO idea about their friends' allowance.

◕ 1 in 4 (24%) know friendship is golden, and their friends get more gold.

◔ 1 in 8 (13%) say they've got the same power—the same spending power as their friends.

◔ And another 1 in 8 (also 13%) are allowed more allowance than their friends are allowed.

WEIRD-O-METER   NO IDEA = 2, ALL OTHER ANSWERS = 3

⁴ 2+1= COMPANY?

DO YOU HAVE ANY FRIENDS WHO ARE TWINS?

"I do! I do! I hang out with both of them," said about 1 in 3 kids (32%).

"I do and I don't! I hang out with only one of them," said more than 1 in 6 kids (15%).

"I don't and I don't!" said more than half of all kids (53%). "But feel free to ask me about quintuplets."

WEIRD-O-METER YES AND YES = 3, YES AND NO = 4, NO AND NO = 2

5 THE BIG SLEEPOVER

HOW OLD WERE YOU WHEN YOU HAD YOUR FIRST OFFICIAL SLEEPOVER? THERE'S REALLY NO NORMAL ANSWER HERE.

Under six? 1 in 5 kids (20%) got an early start on late-night gatherings.

Six? 1 in 9 (11%) packed a pillow to go.

Seven? Same (suit)case as six (11%)

Eight? That's the likeliest sleepover year, with 1 in 7 (14%) saying "good night" to someone else's folks.

Nine is ten (10%), meaning 1 in 10 kids started at that age.

Ten? Super! You're 1 in 16 (6%) staying up, up, and away.

Eleven? (3%) Twelve? (2%) Over 12? (3%) You may be starting a little later, but you're staying up a lot later.

Never slept over? You may sleep alone, but you're not alone. 1 in 5 (20%) haven't had a sleepover yet.

WEIRD-O-METER LESS THAN 6 = 2, 6-7 = 3, 8 = 2, 9 = 3, 10 AND UP = 4, NEVER HAD ONE = 2

6 DID YOU EVEN SLEEP?

How did your first "away" sleepover end?

71%

Most of the time, most of the kids actually slept over on their sleepover.

5%

1 in 20 made that middle-of-the-night phone call, but they almost made it.

4%

Just 1 in 25 kids headed home before heads hit the pillow.

20%

And 1 in 5 kids haven't had one. Because, after all, what's better than your own bed?

WEIRD-O-METER STAYED = 1, LEFT IN THE MIDDLE OF THE NIGHT/LEFT BEFORE BEDTIME = 4, HAVEN'T HAD ONE YET = 3

51

7

DOOM
UNTO OTHERS?

WHAT DO YOU DO IF SOMEONE IS RUDE TO YOU?

1 in 6 kids (17%) say "sticks and stones" and ignore those . . . those . . . people.

1 in 8 kids (12%) send the rudeness right back to the offender.

1 in 10 kids (10%) are all sugar and spice and plenty nice whenever someone gets all spicy in their face.

And the rest? A mere much-more-than-half (61%) said it depends on how rude a person is. They're nice until that rude person crosses the line, wherever that line may be.

Sorry

WEIRD-O-METER IGNORE = 3, RUDE BACK = 4, NICE BACK = 4, IT DEPENDS ON THE SITUATION = 2

8 DUDE, MEET... UM!... OTHER DUDE?

Ever forget someone's name? If you aren't embarrassed to ask, you're not alone.

- **4 out of 10 kids (40%)** say, "I'm sorry, what'd your parents name you again?"

But if you ARE embarrassed for some reason here are the three top tactics to game that name:

- **SNEAK IT:** 21% try something clever like "Hey, let me see your library card . . ."
- **WHISPER IT:** 21% mumble "Quick, whozat?" in a friend's ear, hoping for an answer.
- **FAKE IT:** 18% go for "So, which way do you spell your name again?" Warning: The answer to that one could be "B-O-B."

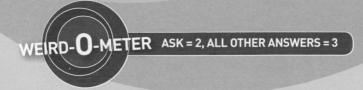

WEIRD-O-METER   ASK = 2, ALL OTHER ANSWERS = 3

WHERE ARE YOU ON THE WEIRD-O-METER?

ADD UP YOUR SCORE AND YOU'LL GET A WEIRDNESS NUMBER THAT WILL MAKE YOUR **FRIENDS** JEALOUS.

YOU'RE AS NORMAL AS STARTING A CLUB WITH YOUR FRIENDS.

Friends and you go together like spaghetti and meatballs. You'll stand up for your friends, but you don't always stand out in the crowd. That's okay— it's tiring to stand all the time! But you don't sit down on the job, either. You're a friend indeed, and it shows. You have good ones, you have great ones, and you've got spare ones. And yeah, you've got annoying ones. But that's why you're such a friend.

20–24

YOU'RE AS NORMAL AS STARTING A PUPPET THEATER WITH YOUR FRIENDS.

So, you like hanging out sometimes, but not always? It depends on the people, and it depends on the plans. You go with the flow, yet you go your own way, too. If the who, what, where, why, and when work for you, you're in. You don't ruffle feathers because you're your own bird, and people respect you for it. There's nothing wrong with that.

25–29

YOU'RE AS NORMAL AS STARTING AN AIRLINE WITH YOUR FRIENDS.

Some people march to the beat of their own drummer. You don't march, you drive a tank. When you're in, you're really in. When you're out, you're way out. Go with the flow? When you do, you're white-water rafting with the gang. When you don't, you're the Hoover Dam. With friendships and you, normal rules don't apply. But that's only because, in this case, you're not normal!

30

40

THAT'S SOOO NOT NORMAL!

MATCH THE NOT-SO-NORMAL HABIT TO THE TIME AND PLACE WHERE IT WAS PERFECTLY NORMAL.

1. **WEARING ANIMAL FURS ALL WINTER AND GOING NAKED IN THE SUMMER**

2. **WIPING YOUR BOTTOM WITH A SPONGE ON A STICK**

3. **GOING TO THE BATHROOM IN A POT AND EMPTYING IT OUT THE WINDOW**

4. **WALKING AROUND WEARING FOOT-HIGH STILTS ON YOUR FEET**

5. **WEARING THE SAME UNDERWEAR FOR MONTHS WITHOUT WASHING IT . . . OR YOURSELF**

6. **SLEEPING ON A BED OF ICE IN A ROOM MADE OF ICE**

7. **HAVING A REALLY LONG FINGERNAIL ON YOUR PINKY**

A. Ye olde London—14th century

B. Arctic Circle—21st century

C. Ancient Rome—1000 B.C.

D. Lebanon—14th–17th centuries

E. Paleolithic Era—10,000 B.C.

F. China and other parts of Asia—21st century

G. Wild West, U.S.A.—19th century

ANSWERS: 1: E, 2: C, 3: A, 4: D, 5: G, 6: B, 7: F

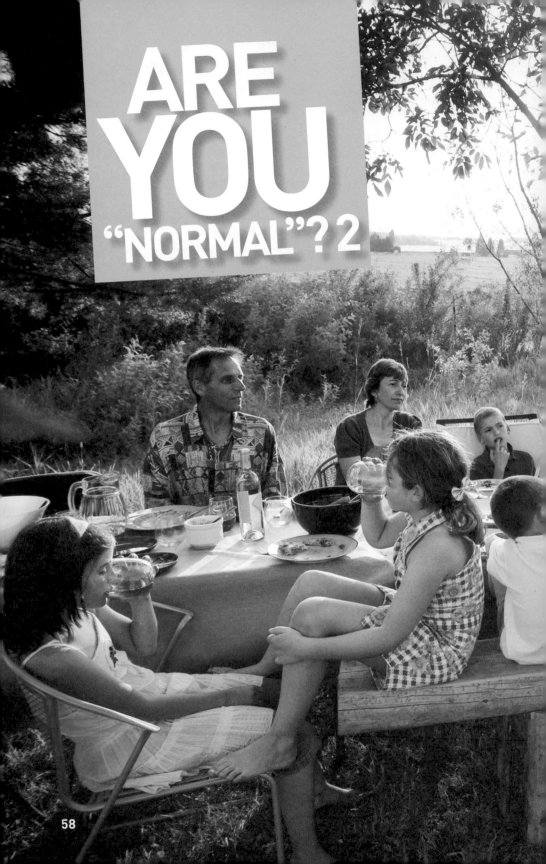

ARE YOU "NORMAL"? 2

FAMILY

FAMILY QUIZ

BE SURE TO KEEP TRACK OF YOUR ANSWERS!

1 WOULD YOU SAY YOU ARE FRIENDS WITH YOUR SIBLINGS?

- Yes, okay friends
- Yes, good friends
- I like some but not all.
- No, I need new siblings.
- I don't have any siblings.

2 DO YOU CALL SOMEONE "AUNT" OR "UNCLE" WHO ISN'T A RELATIVE?

- No
- Yes

3 DO YOU SHARE CLOTHES WITH YOUR SIBLINGS OR FRIENDS?

- No way!
- Yep!

4 HOW MUCH TIME DO YOU SPEND WITH YOUR COUSINS?

- Not much time
- Some time
- A lot of time
- Never see them
- I don't have cousins.

5 HOW OFTEN DO YOU GET WHAT YOU WANT FROM YOUR GROWN-UPS?

- Always
- Usually
- Occasionally
- Rarely
- Never

6 WHAT'S YOUR MAJOR GRIPE AGAINST YOUR GROWN-UPS AT HOME?

- Don't pay enough attention to me
- Don't spend enough time with me
- Don't give me free time
- Too strict
- Don't let me make my own decisions
- Don't give me enough responsibility
- Don't cook what I want
- Don't take me where I want to go
- Something else entirely

7 WHO USUALLY DRIVES THE CAR WHEN THE WHOLE FAMILY IS TOGETHER?

- Dad
- Mom
- Brother
- Sister
- Someone else

8 WHERE DO YOU LIKE TO SIT IN THE CAR?

- In the front
- Behind the front passenger
- In the way back
- Behind the driver
- In the middle

1 BFFs WITH YOUR B & S?

WOULD YOU SAY YOU ARE FRIENDS WITH YOUR SIBLINGS?

WEIRD-O-METER YES/THEY'RE OKAY = 2, ALL OTHER ANSWERS = 3

GOOD NEWS FOR PARENTS: 2 out of 3 kids say they're great, good, or okay friends with their sibs. Here's the scoop:

28% have a houseful of good, built-in buds.

30% say OK, the kids are all right. Sorta.

12% would keep a few, trade a few.

18% want a total reboot. How are they going to do that?

And 12% responded they don't have any brothers or sisters at all. Maybe they can trade with the kids who are unhappy with their sibs?

2

WHO'S UP YOUR FAMILY TREE?

WEIRD-O-METER YES = 3, NO = 2

DO YOU CALL SOMEONE "AUNT" OR "UNCLE" WHO ISN'T A RELATIVE? HALF DO, HALF DON'T.

OR MORE PRECISELY, 48% DO AND 52% DON'T HAVE A NON-RELATIVE THEY CALL "AUNT" OR "UNCLE."

3 SHARE WHAT YOU WEAR?

Do you share clothes with your siblings or friends?

A bit more than half (55%) say they never share shirts, pass along pants, and/or dress in the same dress.

And a bit less than half (45%) enjoy sharing a closet full of clothes.

WEIRD-O-METER NO = 2, YES = 3

4 COUSINS
IN THE HOUSE?

How much time do you spend with your cousins?

➤ Your house is **BUZZIN'** with cousins! 1 in 5 agree.

➤ **SOMETIMES** you spend quality time. 1 in 3 say so.

➤ Another 1 in 3 **DON'T SPEND MUCH TIME** on the other side of the family tree.

➤ 1 in 10 **NEVER** see any cousins.

➤ And just 1 in 50 kids say they have **NO COUSINS** at all.

WEIRD-O-METER LOTS OF TIME = 3, SOMETIMES/LITTLE TIME = 2, NEVER = 4, NO COUSINS = 4

5 GET WHAT YOU WANT FROM YOUR GROWN-UPS?

You put in your requests, your orders, your demands . . . you even say please. But how often do the big guys say yes?

Always! 1 in 10 kids (10%) get what they want, when they want.

Usually! 1 in 3 (29%) score more often than not.

Occasionally! More than 1 in 3 kids (36%) get some things sometimes.

Rarely? Nearly 1 in 5 kids (18%) say their wishes are mostly unfulfilled.

Never? Grumble. 7% get nuthin'. (Seriously? Never?)

WEIRD-**O**-METER ALWAYS = 3, USUALLY/OCCASIONALLY = 2, RARELY = 3, NEVER = 4

IMPERFECT PARENTS?

6 WHAT'S YOUR MAJOR GRIPE AGAINST YOUR GROWN-UPS AT HOME? SEEMS LIKE THERE'S A LOT TO COMPLAIN ABOUT.

THEY DON'T:

. . . let you decide to make your own decisions **(14%)**.

. . . make time to spend enough time with you **(10%)**.

. . . free you up to have enough free time **(9%)**.

. . . loosen up, because they're too strict **(9%)**.

. . . pay you the attention you've earned **(6%)**.

. . . act responsibly and give you more responsibility **(5%)**.

. . . cook meals that appeal **(5%)**.

. . . take you where you want to be taken **(5%)**.

MOST IMPORTANT, 1 in 3 kids (30%) say their adults don't do some other thing that's not on this list, but whatever it is, it must be absolutely, vitally important. Right?

WEIRD-O-METER

MAKE YOUR OWN DECISIONS = 2, SPEND ENOUGH TIME/GIVE YOU FREE TIME/TOO STRICT/PAY ATTENTION = 3, NOT ON THIS LIST = 2, ALL OTHER ANSWERS = 4

7 THE WHEEL FACTS OF LIFE

WHO USUALLY DRIVES THE CAR WHEN THE WHOLE FAMILY IS TOGETHER?

- **DAD'S** the driver in **71%** of families.

- **MOM'S** the main motorist in **24%** of homes. Well, not inside the homes . . .

- **SOMEBODY ELSE** holds the keys? That's the way **4%** of families are driven.

- **BROTHERS (1%)** and **SISTERS (1%)** regularly take the wheel. Which is the same as almost never. You can ask, but you know the odds.

WEIRD-O-METER DAD = 1, MOM = 2, SOMEONE ELSE/SIS/BRO = 4

8 PICK A SEAT.
ANY SEAT.
Where do you like to sit in the car?

48% Nearly half of kids prefer a front seat, when and if they're allowed.

Can't make the case for up-front seating? The rest of the seats divvy up pretty evenly.

15% buckle up behind the front passenger.

14% say, "Row three for me."

13% head for the back of the driver's head.

10% aim straight down the middle seat.

REMEMBER: No matter where you sit, you're all going to get there at the same time.

WEIRD-O-METER   FRONT SEAT = 2, ALL OTHER ANSWERS = 3

WHERE ARE YOU ON THE WEIRD-O-METER?

ADD UP YOUR SCORE AND SEE HOW YOU STACK UP AGAINST YOUR SIBLINGS.

YOU'RE AS NORMAL AS LIVING WITH AN ADULT.

If you're here, you might have the kind of family photo they sell with picture frames. Or it looks like that kind of family. Aunts, uncles, and cousins probably wander in and out—sometimes they're even invited! It's the usual give-and-take of people tossed into the same house. There are great days and there are less-great days, but it's all one big normal family.

19–23

YOU'RE AS NORMAL AS LIVING WITH THREE ADULTS.

Ever feel like your home is the set of a play? And you wonder what was going on in the writer's head? You're one of the kids who can't predict what's going to happen next at home. Could be amazing. Could be surprising. Could be just plain ridiculous. Either way, one day you're going to tell these stories about your family and just shake your head and wonder. Until then, there's always private time in your bedroom.

24–28

YOU'RE AS NORMAL AS LIVING WITH A SPORTS TEAM.

Home on the range? Or the deranged? Things may be stranger, but at least there's no danger. Just people and experiences that don't seem like they happen to anyone else. Normal? What's that mean? Grab a camera and pen and start writing all this stuff down . . . one day you're going to create your own story, and you'll want all this crazy material! Otherwise, nobody will believe you.

30

40

ARE YOU "NORMAL"? 2

MONEY

MONEY QUIZ

BE SURE TO KEEP TRACK OF YOUR ANSWERS!

1 WHAT DO YOU USUALLY DO WITH YOUR MONEY?
- Spend a little, save a little
- Save it to get something big
- Spend it soon
- Give it to someone else

2 DO YOU EVER DO JOBS AROUND THE HOUSE TO EARN MONEY?
- No
- Hardly ever
- Sometimes
- Often

3 WHAT KIND OF CHORES DO YOU DO TO EARN MONEY?
- Cleaning up
- Mowing or raking the lawn
- Gardening
- Fixing things
- Painting
- Something else
- I don't do chores.

4 DO YOU BABYSIT FOR MONEY?
- Yes, often
- Yes, sometimes
- Not yet, but I will when I get the chance.
- I'm no babysitter.

5 HAVE YOU EVER SOLD DRINKS OR FOOD IN FRONT OF YOUR HOME?
- No
- A few times
- Often

6 WHERE DO YOU STASH YOUR CASH?
- In a wallet
- In a piggy bank
- In a drawer
- Under the bed
- In a regular bank
- Somewhere else
- I'll never tell.

7 HOW OFTEN DO YOU GET AN ALLOWANCE?
- Every week
- Every 2 weeks
- Every month
- After I earn it
- I don't get an allowance.

8 WHAT'S YOUR FIRST CHOICE FOR SPENDING YOUR MONEY?
- Something I can keep
- Something I can eat
- Something I can do
- Something else

9 WHAT'S THE MOST AMOUNT OF MONEY YOU'VE EVER HAD AT ONE TIME?
- Between $0 and $20
- Between $20 and $50
- Between $50 and $100
- Between $100 and $200
- Between $200 and $300
- Between $300 and $400
- Between $400 and $500
- More than $500

10 WHAT WOULD YOU DO IF YOU FOUND A STRANGER'S WALLET?
- Spend the money in it
- Give it to an adult
- Look for the owner
- Something else

1 WHERE DO THE DOLLARS GO?

What do you usually do with your money?

If you bank it, you can bank on being normal. Nearly 7 in 8 kids (87%) save at least part of the money they get.

Here's the piggy bank breakdown:

44% save part and spend the rest.

43% save it all for something special.

10% spend it soon after they get it.

And 3% hand it over to somebody else.

WEIRD-O-METER   SAVE PART/SAVE ALL = 2, SPEND ALL = 4, HAND IT OVER = 4

2 YOU'VE GOT TO LEARN TO EARN!

DO YOU EVER DO JOBS AROUND THE HOUSE TO EARN MONEY?

When it comes to money, about half of kids would rather work for it than wait for it.

Often didn't happen too often. Just 1 in 7 kids yearn to earn.

Some said sometimes. 1 in 3 are part-time workers.

If you said hardly ever, you're hardly alone. More than 1 in 5 kids are lounging around with you.

And nearly 1 in 3 said yes . . . to NO chores.

WEIRD-O-METER   OFTEN/HARDLY EVER = 3,
SOMETIMES/NEVER = 2

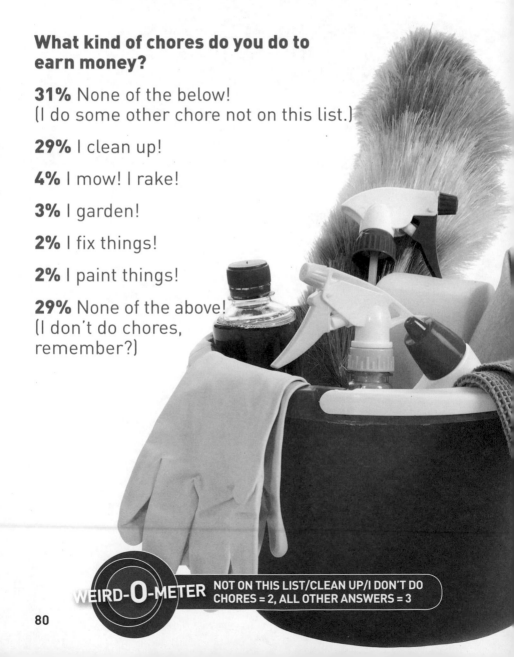

3 THREE CHEERS FOR CHORES!

What kind of chores do you do to earn money?

31% None of the below!
(I do some other chore not on this list.)

29% I clean up!

4% I mow! I rake!

3% I garden!

2% I fix things!

2% I paint things!

29% None of the above!
(I don't do chores,
remember?)

WEIRD-**O**-METER NOT ON THIS LIST/CLEAN UP/I DON'T DO
CHORES = 2, ALL OTHER ANSWERS = 3

4 DO YOU BABYSIT FOR MONEY?

→ **1 IN 20** HAVE A REGULAR GIG WITH YOUNGER KIDS.

→ **1 IN 7** SAY SOMETIMES THEY TAKE CHARGE OF THE CHILDREN.

→ A LOT OF KIDS—MORE THAN **1 IN 3**— HAVEN'T STARTED YET, BUT SOMEDAY, SOMEDAY, THE GROWN-UPS WILL FINALLY GO OUT.

→ AND MORE THAN **1 IN 3** SAY, "LEAVE YOUR SWEET, PRECIOUS, MESSY, NOISY, STICKY KIDS WITH ME? ARE YOU LOCO? THAT'S A NO!"

JUST REMEMBER, YOU DON'T ACTUALLY SIT ON THEM!

WEIRD-**O**-METER   OFTEN = 4, SOMETIMES = 3, NOT YET = 2, NO WAY = 2

5 TODAY, THE DRIVEWAY. TOMORROW, THE WORLD!

HAVE YOU EVER SOLD DRINKS OR FOOD IN FRONT OF YOUR HOME?

LEMONADE

65% If you haven't sold food out in front, you're way out in front. 13 in 20 kids don't sell . . . they buy.

31% More than a few have sold a few snacks a few times. 6 in 20 kids have fed a hungry hood.

5% And only 1 in 20 peddle edibles often. But keep your eyes on those future business tycoons. They're hungry to make things happen.

CLoSeD

WEIRD-O-METER NO = 1, A FEW TIMES = 3, OFTEN = 4

6 WHERE DO YOU STASH YOUR CASH?

- Secrets scored! 41% of kids wouldn't tell us where they cache their cash.

- Wallets work wonders with 18% of kids.

- Piggy banks hog up the money for another 15%.

- Regular banks—the kind with drive-thru windows—lock up the loot for 12%.

- 4% hide it under the underpants in drawers (those high-security vaults).

- 1% bury their treasure under the bed.

- And 9% store their cents somewhere else.

WEIRD-O-METER I'M NOT TELLING/WALLET/PIGGY BANK = 2, REGULAR BANK = 3, DRAWER/UNDER BED = 4, SOMEWHERE ELSE = 3

7 WHICH DAYS ARE PAYDAY?

How often do you get an allowance?

- **EVERY WEEK?** 20% get less, more often.

- **EVERY TWO WEEKS?** Just 4% get it every other week.

- **EVERY MONTH?** 11% make their money monthly.

- **AFTER YOU EARN IT?** 20% call it a paycheck instead.

- **NO ALLOWANCE?** While you may not like it, it's absolutely normal for nearly half (45%) of kids.

WEIRD-O-METER WEEKLY = 2, EVERY TWO WEEKS = 4, MONTHLY = 3, WHEN I EARN IT = 2, I DON'T GET ALLOWANCE = 2

8 SPEND IT? HOW?

GIVEN, SAVED, EARNED, OR FOUND ... WHAT'S YOUR FIRST CHOICE FOR SPENDING YOUR MONEY?

- Something real you can feel? Almost 1 in 2 want a thing they can keep.

- Something edible that's incredible? About 1 in 7 would rather buy something tasty.

- Something new to do? Another 1 in 7 say if they have to buy a ticket, they'll pick it.

- Something not listed (you missed it!)? 1 in 4 said whatever they'd pay for isn't edible, own-able, or do-able. Okay, we give up. What is it?

WEIRD-O-METER KEEP = 2, EAT/DO = 3, SOMETHING ELSE = 2

9 DID THAT PILE MAKE YOU SMILE?

What's the MOST amount of MONEY you've EVER HAD at one time?

Between $0 and $20	10%
Between $20 and $50	9%
Between $50 and $100	16%
Between $100 and $200	20%
Between $200 and $300	12%
Between $300 and $400	6%
Between $400 and $500	7%
More than $500	20%
Total	100%

WEIRD-O-METER $0–$20 = 3, $20–$50 = 3, $50–$100 = 2, $100–$200 = 2, $200–$300 = 3, $300–$400 = 4, $400–$500 = 4, $500+ = 2

I FOUND A FORTUNE?

WHAT WOULD YOU DO
IF YOU FOUND A STRANGER'S WALLET?

➤ "I'd look for the owner," said 1 in 3 kids.

➤ "I'd spend what I found," said 1 in 4 kids.

➤ "I'd give it to an adult," said 1 in 5 kids.

➤ "I'd do something else entirely," said 1 in 6 kids.

WEIRD-**O**-METER LOOK FOR OWNER/SPEND IT = 2,
GIVE TO ADULT/SOMETHING ELSE = 3

WHERE ARE YOU ON THE WEIRD-O-METER?

ADD UP YOUR SCORE AND YOU'LL GET A WEIRDNESS NUMBER THAT NOT EVEN MONEY CAN BUY.

YOU'RE AS NORMAL AS A ONE-DOLLAR BILL.

You work a little, you save a little, you spend a little. You'll make a dollar when the chance comes, but you aren't ready to start your empire just yet. If you like something, maybe you'll save to get it—but you're just as likely to try something tried-and-true, like asking, or begging, or asking again. And if that doesn't work, you might just ask and beg a little louder.

YOU'RE AS NORMAL AS A TWO-DOLLAR BILL.

Got an idea to get rich? You're more likely to give it a try and go the extra mile for the extra dollar. Make a sale, make some lemonade, make a buck. On the other hand, it's possible you'd much rather watch TV than watch your savings grow. In that case, you would probably rather get your money the old-fashioned way: find it on the ground. Hey, why do you think they call them "chores"?

YOU'RE AS NORMAL AS A SEVENTEEN-DOLLAR BILL.

Financially speaking, you're definitely not normal. Maybe money just doesn't matter to you. Or maybe you'd rather make trades with salt and beads, like our ancestors did. Or who knows? Ever wonder what a future millionaire was like as a kid? Well, take a look in the mirror. If a penny saved is a penny earned, you're going to need a pig-sized piggy bank for the sixty tons of pennies you'll be earning and saving.

ARE YOU "NORMAL"? 2

BODY

BODY QUIZ

BE SURE TO KEEP
TRACK OF YOUR
ANSWERS!

1 HOW DO YOU USUALLY SLEEP?
- On your side
- On your stomach
- On your back
- It changes every night.

2 DO PEOPLE HAVE TO REMIND YOU TO FLUSH THE TOILET?
- Never
- Sometimes
- A lot

3 DO YOU CRACK YOUR KNUCKLES?
- Never
- Sometimes
- Yes, all the time

4 CAN YOU DO A CARTWHEEL?
- Yes
- Sort of
- No
- I've never tried.

5 DO YOU LIKE YOUR AGE?
- I like my age just fine.
- I'd rather be younger.
- I'd rather be an older kid.
- I'd rather be an adult.

6 WOULD YOU RATHER TAKE A BATH OR A SHOWER?
- Shower
- Bath
- Ugh! Bathing? No thank you!

7 HAVE YOU EVER BROKEN A BONE?
- No
- Yes, one
- Yes, a few

8 IS YOUR SECOND TOE LONGER THAN YOUR BIG TOE?
- Yes
- No

9 ON WHICH SIDE OF YOUR HEAD DO YOU PART YOUR HAIR?
- In the middle
- On the left
- On the right
- Are you kidding? Have you seen my hair?

10 HOW MANY TIMES A DAY DO YOU BRUSH YOUR TEETH?
- Once
- Twice
- Three times
- After I eat anything
- Not at all

93

1

MAKE A BLANKET STATEMENT.

How do you usually sleep?

→ **40% of kids have a bed-side manner—** they prefer to SLEEP ON THEIR SIDE.

→ **11% score BELLY FLOPS on the mattress** every night.

→ **A mere 6% follow doctor's orders and** SLEEP ON THEIR BACK.

→ **And most kids (43%) do bed spins and** CHANGE UP their positions daily. Or nightly.

WEIRD-O-METER   SIDE = 2, BELLY/BACK = 4, IT CHANGES = 2

2 DO PEOPLE HAVE TO REMIND YOU TO FLUSH THE TOILET?

◑ Here's good news for the next in line—2/3 of kids (66%) handle that handle without being told.

◔ A quarter of the kids (25%) said sometimes they flush and sometimes they rush.

◔ And ugh! 9% seem to think hygiene is just something you say to a guy named Gene. People like a surprise, but not that surprise.

WEIRD-O-METER NO = 2, SOMETIMES = 3, YES = 4

3

CRACK!

DO YOU CRACK YOUR KNUCKLES?

HERE'S HOW THE CRACKING STACKS UP:

➤ HAVEN'T YOU HEARD? NEARLY 3 OUT OF 10 KIDS (28%) **ALWAYS** LET THEIR FINGERS DO THE TALKING.

➤ ABOUT 4 IN 10 (39%) SAY **"SOMETIMES."**

➤ AND MORE THAN 3 IN 10 (33%) SAY **"NO THANKS,** RUINED KNUCKLES INTERFERE WITH MY CLASSICAL PIANO TRAINING AND ANTIQUE CLOCK REPAIR SKILLS."

WEIRD-O-METER YES = 3, SOMETIMES/NO = 2

4

FLIP OUT!

CAN YOU DO A CARTWHEEL?

When it comes to cartwheels, many kids are
head over heels about going head over heels.

YES: ABOUT 1 IN 3 KIDS SAY, HANDS
DOWN, THEY CAN DO A CARTWHEEL.

SORT OF: MORE THAN 1 IN 3 SAY
THEIR WHEEL IS SORT OF LOPSIDED.

NO: NEARLY 1 IN 4 KIDS FLOP WHEN
IT'S THEIR TURN TO FLIP.

NEVER TRIED: MORE THAN 1 IN 12
HAVEN'T PUT THEIR HANDS ON THE
GROUND, THEIR FEET IN THE AIR, AND
THEIR STOMACHS IN THEIR THROATS—
YET.

WEIRD-O-METER YES/SORT OF = 2, NO = 3,
NEVER TRIED = 4

5 DO YOU LIKE YOUR AGE?

Feeling too young? Nearly 1 in 5 kids (18%) want to be older. But not adult-old.

Only 1 in 20 (5%) actually **want to be adults,** probably so they can drive themselves to laser tag—and afford it.

Want fewer candles on your cake? About 1 in 5 (19%) have a **hunger to be younger.**

And the majority by far—well over half (58%)— said they **don't want to change** their age. Until their next birthday, that is.

WEIRD-O-METER OLDER (BUT NOT TOO OLD) = 3, ADULT = 4, YOUNGER = 3, MY AGE IS JUST FINE = 2

6 HOW DO YOU UNDO THE DIRT?

WOULD YOU RATHER TAKE A BATH OR A SHOWER?

- Showers really cleaned up. 63% of kids stand up for soap and water.

- Like to bathe in the bath? About 28% would rather fill it up to wash it off.

- What's that smell? It might be the 9% who don't like baths or showers. Hopefully, they're on the swim team.

WEIRD-O-METER   SHOWER = 2, BATH = 3, NEITHER = 4

7 EVER BROKEN A BONE?

SNAP! 1 in 6 kids (16%) came home from the doctor with some kind of prize: a cast, a sling, a boot, or maybe even some awesome crutches!

SNAP! SNAP! 1 in 11 kids (9%) have broken more than one bone. Hopefully, not both legs at the same time.

NOPE! Most kids—precisely 3 in 4 (75%)—haven't had the pleasure of wearing a cast. But there's always time. Look both ways!

WEIRD-O-METER YES, ONE = 3, YES, MORE THAN ONE = 4, NOPE, NEVER = 1

8 TOE TWO TOO BIG?

Is your second toe longer than your big toe? Sorry: You don't qualify as a mutant. There are way too many like you.

67%
2 out of 3 kids say their big toe IS their big toe.

33%
The remaining 1 in 3 say their second toe is their longer toe, and while that's confusing, it's not really weird.

WEIRD-O-METER BIG TOE IS BIGGER = 2, SECOND TOE IS BIGGER = 3

9 PART YOUR HAIR?
WHERE?

On which side of your head do you part your hair?
(Hint: Don't use a mirror. Touch it with your hand to tell right from left.)

Part it on the left?
Stand in line with 22% of the kids with combs.

Part it on the right?
That's how 17% start their part. (And chances are, you're left-handed.)

Part it down the middle?
Your head may be split, but you're in the majority. 38% have well-balanced hairlines.

No part? Take heart! A lot of kids—23%—have some sort of hairdo that doesn't show any inner skin at all.

WEIRD-O-METER LEFT/RIGHT = 3, MIDDLE = 2, NO PART = 3

10 RUSH TO BRUSH?

How many times a day do you brush your teeth?

- 20% **Once a day?** Better once than never!

- 53% **Twice a day?** Start and end the day in style!

- 13% **Three times a day?** Your smile makes people smile!

- 7% **After you eat anything?** You're a chompers champ!

- 7% **Don't brush at all?** Who needs teeth!

WEIRD-O-METER ONCE A DAY = 3, TWICE = 2, THREE TIMES = 3, AFTER EATING/DON'T BRUSH = 4

WHERE ARE YOU ON THE WEIRD-O-METER?

ADD UP YOUR SCORE AND YOU'LL GET A WEIRDNESS NUMBER THAT WILL MAKE YOU DO **CARTWHEELS.**

YOU'RE AS NORMAL AS USING SHAMPOO.

You might stand out for your hobbies, or your schoolwork, or your athletic abilities. What doesn't stand out is your smell. Bravo! Keeping it together doesn't mean you're just another clone. Everyone's got something original. Lots of people crack knuckles—but on their toes? Or their friends' toes? When it comes to adding new habits to your life, you'll sleep on it . . . and probably sleep a different way every night.

YOU'RE AS NORMAL AS USING CONDITIONER.

Maybe you do cartwheels. Maybe you flush. But for goodness sake, not at the same time! You like yourself just fine, even with those rough edges. Everyone's got 'em. Yours are just a bit more noticeable. A fork is nearly as good as a comb. And isn't it great to be noticed? To be a little not-normal is a great way to make friends. But the occasional bath helps, too. Keep up the good work!

YOU'RE AS NORMAL AS USING ORANGE HAIR DYE.

Welcome to the extremes. You're here because you might be really sloppy, or really neat. Super athletic, or super sluggish. If your second toe isn't eleven feet long, then maybe you've broken it eleven times. Whatever weirdness got you here, wear it as a badge of pride. Anyone can be a well-washed, properly combed, stomach-sleeping knuckle cracker. But it takes a unique person to be all that and remember to flush the toilet. You're amazing!

IS YOUR FAVORITE FOOD NORMAL?

THAT DEPENDS ON WHAT YOUR NEIGHBORS EAT.

DO COOKED GRASSHOPPERS GET YOU HOPPING?

If you live in Mexico, crunching these critters is normal. They're called *chapulines.*

SLURP EARTHWORM SOUP?

In China, it's normal to ladle up this slithery soup when you have a fever.

CHOMP ON GIANT SPIDERS?

In Venezuela, there's a whole web of people who will normally eat all eight legs.

GOT AN EYE FOR SHEEP'S HEAD?

In Iran, it's called *pacha*. It's normal to cook it slowly but gobble it up.

NOT BUGGED BY CHEESE FILLED WITH MAGGOTS?

In Sardinia, maggot cheese is called *casu marzu*. It's illegal, so you normally buy it from criminals.

WANT A MEAL THAT TASTES YOU, TOO?

In Lapland, eating reindeer tongue is so normal, it's what boyfriends give girlfriends to show they care.

LIKE TO UNWIND WITH A SNAIL DINNER?

That's normal in France and Greece. But it's not fast food.

MECHANICALLY SEPARATED POULTRY PASTE SOUND DELICIOUS TO YOU?

WELL IF YOU'RE A KID IN THE UNITED STATES, CHANCES ARE YOU'VE TRIED IT. IT'S A MAIN INGREDIENT IN HOT DOGS.

ARE YOU "NORMAL"? 2

TECH

TECH QUIZ

BE SURE TO KEEP
TRACK OF YOUR
ANSWERS!

1 HOW DO YOU MOSTLY WATCH MOVIES AT HOME?

- On a TV using DVDs
- On a TV connected to the Internet
- On a TV using a DVR
- On a TV using VHS tapes
- On a computer screen
- On a tablet
- I don't watch movies at home.

2 HOW MANY HOURS A WEEK DO YOU SPEND SURFING THE INTERNET?

- 0
- 1–2
- 3–4
- 5–6
- 7–8
- 9–10
- More than 10

3 WHAT KINDS OF PHONES DO YOU HAVE IN YOUR HOME?

- Regular phone and cell phone
- Cell phones only
- Regular phone only
- No phones at all

4 DO YOU EVER LOOK TO SEE WHO'S CALLING AND NOT ANSWER THE PHONE?

- Sometimes
- All the time
- Never

5 HOW MANY TVs ARE IN YOUR HOME?

- 0
- 1
- 2
- 3
- 4
- 5
- 6
- 7

6 COULD SOMEONE WHO KNOWS YOU WELL GUESS YOUR ONLINE PASSWORD?

- Nope, security is as tight as Fort Knox.
- Maybe
- I don't have any online passwords.
- Yes, I'm an open book!

7 DO YOU HAVE YOUR OWN EMAIL ACCOUNT?

- Yes
- No, I don't use email.
- No, I use someone else's.
- Yes, but I'm not supposed to.

8 DO YOU USE THE SAME ONLINE NICKNAME?

- Sometimes
- All the time
- I don't use one.
- I always change it.

9 DOES ANYONE EVER MAKE YOU SHUT DOWN YOUR GADGETS AND PLAY OUTSIDE?

- Sometimes
- Nope, everyone leaves me alone.
- Yes, all the time

10 HOW OLD WERE YOU WHEN YOU GOT YOUR OWN CELL PHONE?

- 15 or older
- 14
- 13
- 12
- 11
- 10
- 9
- 8
- 7
- 6
- 5 or younger
- Don't have a phone

1 A MOVIE IS GROOVY, BUT... ON WHAT?

HOW DO YOU MOSTLY WATCH MOVIES AT HOME?

- ◑ **48%** TV with DVDs
- ◔ **15%** TV with the Internet
- ◕ **14%** TV with a DVR
- ◔ **2%** TV with VHS tapes
- ◔ **11%** Computer
- ◔ **4%** Tablet
- ◔ **6%** No movies at home

WEIRD-**O**-METER DVD = 2, TV WITH INTERNET/DVR/COMPUTER = 3, VHS/TABLET/NOTHING = 4

2 TIME ONLINE?

How many hours a week do you spend surfing the Internet?

(And a list of what you could do in that time.)

0 HOURS (8%) No time for the net.

1–2 HOURS (26%) Sleep through your two least favorite subjects.

3–4 HOURS (20%) Watch about two movies.

5–6 HOURS (12%) Fly coast to coast (on an airplane).

7–8 HOURS (8%) Get a doctor-recommended, parent-enforced full night's sleep.

9–10 HOURS (7%) Put everything you own in alphabetical order.

10+ (19%) Be awake for an entire day . . . or night.

WEIRD-O-METER 0 HOURS = 3, 1–2 HOURS/3–4 HOURS = 2, 5–6 HOURS/7–8 HOURS = 3, 9–10 HOURS = 4, 10 OR MORE HOURS = 2

3 WHAT'S THAT RINGING IN YOUR EARS?

WHAT KINDS OF PHONES DO YOU HAVE IN YOUR HOME?

- ◖ **MORE PHONES IS MORE NORMAL.** 73% of kids have cell phones and regular phones at home.

- ◔ **JUST A CELL CALL?** Cool. 21% dwell in cell-only homes.

- ◔ **NO CELL . . . HOME PHONE ONLY?** That's getting less normal every day. Only 5% live cell-free.

- ◔ **PHONES?** What are those? 1% have a home with no phone at all.

4 DO U I.D.?

Do you ever look to see who's calling and not answer the phone?

52%
"Sometimes I pick it up, sometimes I pass," say half the kids.

14%
"Hello??? I never do that!!!" say 1 in 7 kids.

34%
"Oh, yeah! Only a few get through," say 1 in 3 kids.

WEIRD-O-METER   SOMETIMES/YES = 2, NO = 4

5 IT'S AS EASY AS 1, T.V.

0 TVs 1 in 50 kids (2%)

1 TV 1 in 5 kids (20%)

2 TVs 1 in 4 kids (27%)

How many TVs are in your home?
(Too bad we didn't ask how many you watch each day.)

3 TVs 1 in 5 kids (22%)

4 TVs 1 in 8 kids (13%)

5 TVs 1 in 11 kids (9%)

6 TVs 1 in 33 kids (3%)

7 TVs or more 1 in 25 kids (4%)

WEIRD-O-METER ZERO TVs = 4, 1 TO 4 TVs = 2, 5 TVs= 3, 6 OR MORE TVs = 4

6 HALT!
WHO GOES THERE?

Could someone who knows you well guess your online password?

➤ **NO WAY!** My password would pass the CIA test—even if you tickle me. (55%)

➤ **MAYBE THEY'D GUESS . . .** I know some pretty smart people. (36%)

➤ **UM, PROBABLY.** As in, probably predictable passwords. (4%)

➤ **PASSWORDS?** I don't have any. No, really! Stop tickling me! (5%)

WEIRD-O-METER NO/MAYBE = 2, YES/NO PASSWORDS = 4

7

YOU@EMAIL.COM

DO YOU HAVE YOUR OWN EMAIL ACCOUNT?

65%
Yes@AbsolutelyHaveMyOwnEmail.com

20%
No@NoEmailAccountAtTheMoment.com

10%
No@UsingTheEmailOf-
SomebodyElse.com

5%
Yes@BeingSneakyAnd-
BreakingTheRules.com

WEIRD-O-METER   ABSOLUTELY = 1, NO = 3, USING SOMEONE
ELSE'S/YES BUT BREAKING RULES = 4

8 DO YOU NICK THE SAME NAME EVERY TIME?

When it comes to user names, do you use the same online nickname?

38% **Sometimes same same same. Sometimes changed, different, original.**

27% **I use the same same same same same name.**

20% **Nickname? I don't use any name online.**

15% **I totally, completely, fully, 100%, absolutely, thoroughly change it.**

WEIRD-O-METER **YES/SOMETIMES = 2, NO/I DON'T USE ONLINE NICKNAMES = 3**

9 STOP PLAYING AND START PLAYING!

DOES ANYONE EVER MAKE YOU SHUT DOWN YOUR GADGETS AND GO PLAY OUTSIDE?

→ **20% OH, YEAH.** I can't boot up a device without getting booted out.

→ **53% SOMETIMES** they let me run my games. Sometimes they make me run my legs.

→ **27% NO,** once I settle in with a gadget, that settles it.

WEIRD-O-METER YES = 3, SOMETIMES = 2, NO = 3

10
CELL PHONE?

How old were you when you got your own?

- 15 OR OLDER: 20%
- 14: 5%
- 13: 9%
- 12: 13%
- 11: 12%
- 10: 15%
- 9: 9%
- 8: 8%
- 7: 3%
- 6: 3%
- 5 OR YOUNGER: 4%

If you don't have one, you're the most normal of all. **More than half** of all school-age kids don't have a cell phone.

WEIRD-O-METER 15 OR OLDER = 2, 14 = 3, 13/12/11/10/9 = 2, 8 = 3, 7/6/5 = 4, NO PHONE = 2

WHERE ARE YOU ON THE WEIRD-O-METER?

ADD UP YOUR SCORE AND YOU'LL GET A WEIRDNESS NUMBER YOU CAN **PLUG** INTO.

1–24

YOU'RE AS NORMAL AS A TOUCH-SCREEN TABLET.

Whether you spend a few hours on the Internet, or watch a few movies (on a few televisions), the key word is "few." Not too much, not too little, not too wired, and not wireless. Keeping up with tech is normal for you, but so is going out, hanging out, and other activities where batteries aren't included . . . or required.

YOU'RE AS NORMAL AS A TOUCH-SCREEN TV.

You know your way around the Internet, and you're smart about websites and email. There's also a good chance your house at night has little blue and red glowing dots all over the place. They help you find your way in the dark. But what you can't find is an unused outlet. You've got so much stuff plugged in, your walls look like they're growing roots!

YOU'RE AS NORMAL AS A TOUCH-SCREEN MOVIE THEATER.

Or maybe you're as normal as a drive-in movie theater? Because if you're here, you're either really high-tech or really low voltage. Got 8 TVs going at home, maybe all at the same time? It's also possible you have no TV, and you spend your time the original way: unplugged. Whatever your story, it's not the typical one.

ARE YOU "NORMAL"? 2

FOOD

FOOD QUIZ

BE SURE TO KEEP TRACK OF YOUR ANSWERS!

1 WHEN DINNER IS OVER, WHAT DO YOU USUALLY DO?
- Finish my meal
- Leave a little on my plate
- Leave a lot on my plate

2 DO YOU FINISH YOUR MEAL AT THE SAME TIME AS YOUR FAMILY?
- I'm slower.
- I'm faster.
- We all finish at the same time.

3 WHEN IT'S SNACK TIME, DO YOU GO SWEET OR SALTY?
- I mix it up.
- Usually sweet
- Usually salty

4 ARE YOU ALLERGIC TO NUTS?
- No
- Yes, a little
- Yes, very

5 WHAT'S YOUR #1 FAVORITE THING FOR BREAKFAST?

- Cold cereal
- Hot cereal
- Something fresh
- Nothing
- Something with eggs
- Something in a wrapper
- Something toasted
- Something else

6 DO YOU EAT THE SAME THING FOR BREAKFAST EVERY SCHOOL DAY?

- No
- Nearly always
- Yes

7 DO YOU HAVE A FAVORITE PLATE, BOWL, CUP, OR PIECE OF SILVERWARE?

- Cup
- Silverware
- Bowl
- Plate
- More than one
- I don't have any favorites.

8 WHAT'S YOUR FAVORITE BERRY?

- Strawberry
- Raspberry
- Blueberry
- Blackberry
- Other berry
- No berry

9 WHAT COUNTRY HAS YOUR FAVORITE KIND OF FOOD?

- Italy
- United States
- China
- Japan
- Mexico
- India
- Thailand
- Germany
- Other

10 WHAT KIND OF EATER ARE YOU?

- I'm pretty picky.
- I'm an explorer.
- I'm somewhere in the middle.

1 WHEN DINNER IS OVER, WHAT DO YOU USUALLY DO?

46%
Another almost-half leave a little, presumably for the dog.

47%
About half of kids finish all the food they're given.

7%
And the rest say they leave a lot. Picky eating? Ucky cooking? Or maybe the plates are just really, really big.

WEIRD-O-METER   FINISH ALL = 2, LEAVE A LITTLE = 2, LEAVE A LOT = 4

2

SPEED
EATING?

DO YOU FINISH YOUR MEAL AT THE SAME TIME AS YOUR FAMILY?

- If you do, like nearly 1 in 5 kids (18%), that's kind of weird. How do you do it, exactly? "Forks up, everyone . . . take a bite . . . now chew, chew, CHEW!"
- On the other hand, if you're THE TORTOISE (44%),
- or THE HARE (38%) . . . then you're pretty much normal.

Tell that to the folks trying to rush you.

WEIRD-**O**-METER SAME TIME = 3, FINISH LAST = 2, FINISH FIRST = 2

3 SNACK TIME: SWEET OR SALTY?

Candy, cookies, and cocoa? 1 out of 3 kids (34%) want a sweet treat to eat.

Pretzels, popcorn, and peanuts? 1 out of 7 kids (14%) say salt shakes them up.

But if your mouth wants to munch on a mix—sometimes sweet, sometimes salty—you're in the majority. More than half (52%) hunger for both. How does a chocolate-covered pretzel sound right about now?

WEIRD-O-METER   SWEET = 3, SALTY = 4, MIX OF BOTH = 2

4 NUTS TO YOU?

Are you allergic to nuts?

Allergic to almonds? Worried about walnuts? Maybe not, but chances are someone in your classroom is. That's because 1 in 25 kids **(4%) ARE VERY ALLERGIC** to nuts.

Another 4% **ARE A LITTLE BIT** allergic. Which is nothing to sneeze at.

And the rest—92%—say **"PASS THE PEANUT BUTTER!"**

WEIRD-**O**-METER VERY ALLERGIC/SLIGHTLY ALLERGIC = 4, NOT ALLERGIC = 1

5 TOP OF THE MORNING!

What's your #1 favorite thing for breakfast? The answers are as mixed-up as scrambled eggs.

- 18% are bowled over by cold cereal.
- 13% get fresh with fresh foods.
- 5% get mushy over hot cereal.
- 3% find wrappers appealing.
- 15% say eggs go over easy.
- 12% say a toast to their toaster.
- 5% eat nothing. Not even syrup.
- And the answer that gets the most agreement by far? 3 out of 10 (29%) say, "None of the above." Yum.

WEIRD-O-METER EGGS/COLD CEREAL/SOMETHING FRESH/SOMETHING ELSE = 2, SOMETHING TOASTED = 3, HOT CEREAL/SOMETHING IN A WRAPPER/NOTHING AT ALL = 4

6

WHAT'S FOR BREAKFAST?
Do you eat the same thing every school day?

The majority (57%) take the routine route by always eating the SAME THING EVERY DAY (18%), or nearly always (39%).

Only 43% reach for SOMETHING DIFFERENT on different days.

That's why the cereal boxes get so big.

WEIRD-O-METER ALWAYS = 3, NEARLY ALWAYS = 2, SOMETHING DIFFERENT = 2

7

IT WON'T BE A MEAL WITHOUT . . .

DO YOU HAVE A FAVORITE PLATE, BOWL, CUP, OR PIECE OF SILVERWARE?

- Your favorite cup? 14% of kids have one.

- Special silverware? 9% prefer to hold some.

- That bowl you love? 6% have soup in a super-bowl.

- A V.I.P. (Very Important Plate)? 3% vote for one.

- Use lots of the same things . . . a lot? Join the 13%.

- Chances are, you're one of the people who cares more about the food than the tools. More than half of kids (55%) say, "Just make sure it's clean!"

8 WHAT'S YOUR BERRY FAVORITE?

Black? Blue? Straw? Rasp?
One berry takes the cake.

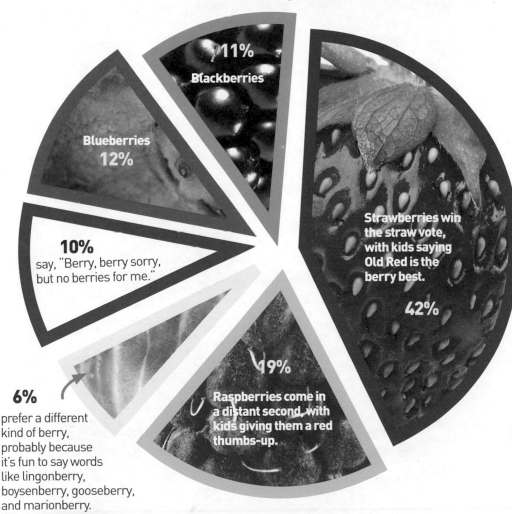

11%
Blackberries

Blueberries
12%

10%
say, "Berry, berry sorry, but no berries for me."

Strawberries win the straw vote, with kids saying Old Red is the berry best.

42%

6%
prefer a different kind of berry, probably because it's fun to say words like lingonberry, boysenberry, gooseberry, and marionberry.

19%
Raspberries come in a distant second, with kids giving them a red thumbs-up.

WEIRD-**O**-METER STRAWBERRY/RASPBERRY = 2, BLUEBERRY/BLACKBERRY/NO BERRY = 3, NOT ON THIS LIST = 4

9 WHERE IN THE WORLD DO YOU WANT TO EAT?

What country has your favorite kind of food?

ITALY 23.5%

UNITED STATES 13.0%

CHINA 12.8%

JAPAN 9.0%

MEXICO 8.6%

INDIA 6.1%

THAILAND 4.4%

GERMANY 4.1%

OTHER 18.4%

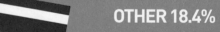

WEIRD-O-METER ITALY/UNITED STATES/CHINA = 2, JAPAN/MEXICO /INDIA = 3, THAILAND/GERMANY = 4, OTHER = 2

10

PACK IT IN OR PICKY?

What kind of eater are you?

Picky people, you're not alone. We hear you, even when your parents yell for you to try something new. More than 1 in 4 kids (28%) have what you might call "specific tastes."

Eating explorers, you're in good company, too. An equal amount of kids (27%) say they're dinner daredevils.

Did you say sometimes you eat it, sometimes you beat it? That puts you in the mealtime majority. Almost half of all kids (45%) take it case by case. Also, it depends on what's for dessert!

WEIRD-O-METER   PICKY = 3, PACK IT IN = 3, DEPENDS = 2

WHERE ARE YOU ON THE WEIRD-O-METER?

ADD UP YOUR SCORE AND YOU'LL GET A WEIRDNESS NUMBER YOU CAN TAKE A BITE OUT OF.

YOU'RE AS NORMAL AS CHOCOLATE CHIP COOKIES.

Hungry for something new? Maybe. Maybe not. You might like an adventure in life, but not really on your plate. Want something particular for dinner? It's a safe bet you've had it before. Maybe recently. Maybe yesterday. That means you know what you like and you stick with your favorites. And best of all, whoever makes your dinners knows what will make you very happy . . . or very unhappy!

25–31

YOU'RE AS NORMAL AS CHOCOLATE CHIP PANCAKES.

Food for you is as unpredictable as a stranger's meat loaf. It all depends. Restaurants? You'll try a new one. Vegetables? They're not all awful. Bottle of sauce? Sure. What if there's something weird on the label? Mmm, weird but good! A little daring goes a long way—and it can get you a five-star dinner or a five-alarm stomachache. But this is food we're talking about, so it's always worth the risk.

32–37

YOU'RE AS NORMAL AS CHOCOLATE CHIP HAMBURGERS.

When you're the one making the food, people run for the hills. Or they run for jumbo forks and spoons. You never know. You're the most unpredictable of eaters. You like your meals at all hours. You like your desserts served on fire. When someone asks what you want to eat, you answer in French. You prefer foods that nobody has eaten, or recognizes, or can spell. It's not normal, but it is—if you're lucky—the most incredible delicacy anyone ever had.

CAN YOU DO THIS?

IF YOU CAN DO THESE THINGS, YOU ARE DEFINITELY NOT NORMAL.

CLOSE YOUR EYES. ROLL YOUR EYEBALLS AS FAR AS YOU CAN UP INTO YOUR SKULL. WITHOUT MOVING YOUR EYEBALLS, OPEN YOUR EYES.

LAY A SINGLE SHEET OF **NEWSPAPER** ON THE FLOOR. WITH ONLY ONE HAND, **CRUMPLE** IT INTO A BALL THAT **FITS IN YOUR HAND.**

TAKE A **TOOTHPICK** IN EACH HAND. **CLOSE ONE EYE** AND GET THE **POINTS TO TOUCH** ON THE FIRST TRY.

PUT A TOOTHPICK ON TOP OF YOUR **MIDDLE FINGER, BETWEEN** YOUR **FINGERNAIL AND FIRST KNUCKLE.** PUT YOUR **POINTER** AND **RING FINGERS** ON TOP OF THE TOOTHPICK. **BREAK** THE TOOTHPICK BY PUSHING UP OR DOWN.

141

ARE YOU "NORMAL"? 2

ME

ME
QUiZ

BE SURE TO KEEP
TRACK OF YOUR
ANSWERS!

1 OTHER THAN EARTH, WHAT'S YOUR FAVORITE PLANET?

- Mercury
- Venus
- Mars
- Ceres
- Jupiter
- Saturn
- Uranus
- Neptune
- Pluto
- Eris
- Haumea
- Makemake

2 IS THERE LIFE ON OTHER PLANETS?

- Yes
- No
- I have no earthly idea.

3 HOW DO YOU FEEL ABOUT BIRTHDAY PARTIES?

- The bigger the better
- Just a few close friends
- Just the family
- Ugh, birthday parties? No thanks.

4 DO YOU SLEEP WITH A FAVORITE THING?

- A stuffed animal
- A blanket
- A doll
- A toy
- Something else special
- Nothing extra

5 HOW MANY STUFFED ANIMALS LIVE IN YOUR ROOM?

- Between 1 and 4
- Between 5 and 10
- Between 10 and 20
- Between 20 and a million
- None

6 IF YOU COULD BE ANY ANIMAL, WHICH WOULD IT BE?

- A mammal
- A bird
- A reptile
- A fish
- An insect
- Something not discovered yet

7 WHERE DO YOU WRITE THE THINGS YOU WANT TO REMEMBER?

- Paper
- A body part
- An electronic device
- I make it someone else's job.
- Something else
- I don't even try.

8 IF YOU COULD, WOULD YOU DYE YOUR HAIR CRAZY COLORS?

- No
- Yes
- Been there, done that.

9 WHAT COLOR WOULD YOU LIKE TO PAINT YOUR ROOM?

- Blue
- Purple
- Green
- Orange
- I'd leave it the way it is.
- Red
- Black
- Yellow
- White

OTHER THAN EARTH, WHAT'S YOUR FAVORITE PLANET?

PLANNING A ROCKET VOYAGE THROUGH OUR SOLAR SYSTEM? HERE ARE THE HOTTEST—AND COOLEST—PLACES.

16% **SATURN**, the top choice, runs rings around the other planets.

15% **MARS** is the second favorite. Do you think it's because of the candy?

14% **PLUTO** may no longer be a full planet, but it's full of admirers.

11% **JUPITER** gives more than 1 in 10 stargazers the biggest bang.

NEPTUNE makes a huge splash with 10% of kids.

MAKEMAKE is a dwarf planet with a fun name—and 9% of astrology admirers.

VENUS is mysteriously beautiful to only 8% of kids.

8% **URANUS** is Saturn's dad in Roman myths, but gets only half of the love.

ERIS, our largest dwarf planet, is 1/4 Earth's size, with barely 3% of the admirers.

HAUMEA, a dwarf 1/3 the size of Pluto, is chosen less than 3% of the time.

MERCURY, our hottest and speediest planet, scored a cold, slow 2%.

1% **CERES**, smallest of the dwarf planets, also has the smallest following.

WEIRD-O-METER SATURN/MARS/PLUTO/JUPITER/NEPTUNE/ MAKEMAKE = 2, VENUS/URANUS = 3, ALL OTHER ANSWERS = 4

2 IS THERE LIFE ON OTHER PLANETS?

UNFORTUNATELY, THE TELESCOPE DOESN'T TELL US MUCH.

YES: Just over half of kids (52%) say we're not alone. Better tidy up. We may get visitors.

NO: About 1 in 5 kids (19%) believe we're unique in the universe.

???: Nearly 1 in 3 (29%) say, "How on Earth should I know?"

WEIRD-**O**-METER   YES = 2, NO = 3, I HAVE NO CLUE = 3

3 HAPPY BIRTHDAY TO YOU!

How do you feel about birthday parties?

- **39% THE BIGGER THE BETTER!** That's the biggest answer. 4 in 10 kids want a big, big cake for the crowd.

- **37% JUST A FEW CLOSE FRIENDS?** That answer's a close second. Nearly 4 in 10 say, "I'll take my party small (but my presents can be big!)."

- **20% FAMILY ONLY?** 2 in 10 would rather keep the party at home.

- **4% NO WAY! NO PARTY!** No thanks. A handful of kids would rather get older gracefully, not publicly.

WEIRD-O-METER BIG/A FEW FRIENDS = 2, JUST FAMILY = 3, NO PARTY = 4

4

GO TO THE HEAD OF THE BED.

Do you sleep with a favorite thing?
If you do, you're not (sleeping) alone. 3 out of 4 kids
say "yes" to having a favorite.

→ More than 1 in 3 kids (41%) say an animal friend that's
fluffy and stuffed is enough.

→ 1 in 7 kids (14%) couldn't find their favorite on this list,
but they can find it in the dark.

→ 1 in 5 kids (19%) want a blanket—no, not that blanket
—a very particular blanket.

→ 1 in 50 (2%) want that doll, and 1 in 100 (1%) want that toy.

→ And 1 in 4 kids (24%) say, "No thanks, I'll fly solo to dreamland."

WEIRD-O-METER STUFFED ANIMAL/BLANKET/NOTHING = 2,
SOMETHING NOT ON THIS LIST = 3, TOY/DOLL = 4

5 GOT STUFFED?

How many stuffed animals live in your room? (Chances are, it's pretty plush.)

🌑 **20 to 1,000,000!** More than 1 in 3 kids (42%) can't bear to live without a whole lot of bears.

🌒 **10 to 20!** 1 in 6 kids (17%) can play school with their critters and set up a pretty good-sized classroom.

🌓 **5 to 10!** 1 in 8 kids (12%) can field a baseball team or basketball team entirely with fuzzy players.

🌔 **1 to 4!** Join the 1 in 6 kids (17%) who can actually carry all their stuffed animals at the same time.

🌕 **None!** Maybe you're one of the 1 in 8 (12%) who doesn't keep stuffed animals . . . but that doesn't mean you haven't set a bunch of them free.

WEIRD-O-METER 20 OR MORE = 2, ALL OTHER ANSWERS = 3

6 GOT THAT ANIMAL URGE?

IF YOU COULD BE ANY ANIMAL, WHICH WOULD IT BE?

Bugs really bugged the most people. Just 1 in 100 (1%) want six legs, wings, and dozens of eyes. Wonder why?

Fish-lovers didn't exactly tip the scales, either. 1 in 33 kids (3%) want to trade fingers for fins.

Reptiles also make most kids' blood run cold. 1 in 20 kids (5%) hope it's easy being green.

Birds soared in the survey. More than 1 in 5 (22%) would like to flock together.

Mammals—cute, furry, big-eyed, sweet, cuddly mammals— are the big favorite. More than 1 in 3 kids (40%) clearly don't want to wander too far into the animal kingdom.

Almost 1 in 3 (29%) want to be some new, undiscovered, possibly mutant species. Of course, that would probably change if that species lived off the scum at the bottom of an old garbage can.

WEIRD-O-METER BUG/FISH/REPTILE = 4, BIRD/MAMMAL/ SOMETHING NOT YET DISCOVERED = 2

7

When you need a reminder . . .
WHAT'S WRITE FOR YOU?

Where do you write things you want to remember?

41% PAPER tore apart the competition! More than 1 in 3 kids reach for a piece.

KEYS?

22% Nearly 1 in 4 write on their **BODY.** Fortunately, they didn't tell us where.

9% 1 in 11 gave a plug for writing on an **ELECTRONIC DEVICE.**

LIGHTS?

WINDOWS?

14% DON'T SCRIBBLE and don't try? Don't worry. 1 in 7 kids would rather think than ink.

WALLET?

STOVE?

4% At least 1 in 25 kids are future business managers. **THEY GIVE THE JOB TO SOMEONE ELSE.**

PHONE?

10% GOT ANOTHER NOTE-TAKING METHOD? So did 1 in 10 kids. They use something like smoke signals, cave paintings, or the big signs in Times Square.

WEIRD-O-METER PAPER/BODY PART = 2, SOMETHING NOT ON THIS LIST/DON'T EVEN TRY = 3, ALL OTHER ANSWERS = 4

8 HAIR YOU GO!

IF YOU COULD, WOULD YOU DYE YOUR HAIR CRAZY COLORS?

54% "ARE YOU KIDDING? NO! Seriously, are you out of your mind? I mean, did you dye your brain or something?" say more than half of kids.

37% "OH, YEAH, MAN. No problem," say more than 1 in 3 kids.

9% "THAT'S OLD NEWS, PAL. Haven't you seen my rainbow hairbrush?" say 1 in 11 kids.

WEIRD-**O**-METER   YES/NO = 2, ALREADY DID = 4

9

COLOR
YOUR WORLD

What color would you like to paint your room? Guess what? Darker colors got the brighter response.

BLUE! More than 1 in 4 kids (28%)

PURPLE! Nearly 1 in 5 kids (18%)

GREEN! About 1 in 7 kids (15%)

ORANGE! Just 1 in 20 kids (5%)

RED! Same as orange! (5%)

BLACK! Same as orange and red! (5%)

Except black isn't even a color.

YELLOW! Only 1 in 25 kids (4%)

WHITE! A mere 1 in 33 kids (3%) picked
the color that's actually all the colors!

"I LIKE MY ROOM THE WAY IT IS!" is a weird name
for a color, but 1 in 6 kids (17%) said so anyway.

WEIRD-O-METER BLUE/PURPLE/GREEN/I LIKE IT THE
WAY IT IS = 2, ALL OTHER ANSWERS = 4

WHERE ARE YOU ON THE WEIRD-O-METER?

ADD UP YOUR SCORE AND YOU'LL GET A WEIRDNESS NUMBER THAT'S TOTALLY YOU.

1–22

YOU'RE AS NORMAL AS WEARING BOOTS IN SNOW.

When it comes to picking your favorite things, you're not too far out there—just like those popular, picturesque planets you probably prefer. Hair color? Probably natural. Room color? Stick with the basics. Stuffed animals? Your room's a zoo, isn't it? For you, it's not the things you surround yourself with that define you . . . it's what's inside!

YOU'RE AS NORMAL AS WEARING SANDALS IN SNOW.

Like to stir things up a little? Why take a rocket when you can go by helicopter to your favorite planet? And when you get there, you're probably hoping to find intelligent life. (Wouldn't that be a nice change?) Bring something special to snuggle on the ride. Being **you** means being un-you-sual . . . and usually, that means bigger, bolder choices.

YOU'RE AS NORMAL AS WEARING ROLLER SKATES IN SNOW.

You're as out-there as the smallest, least known planets. And chances are when it comes to hair color . . . you take chances. You probably don't sleep with a stuffed animal. But a stuffed insect? Or better yet, a living one? Maybe. No matter how you measure it, your tastes make you totally **you**-nique. Who needs safe choices when wild ones will do?

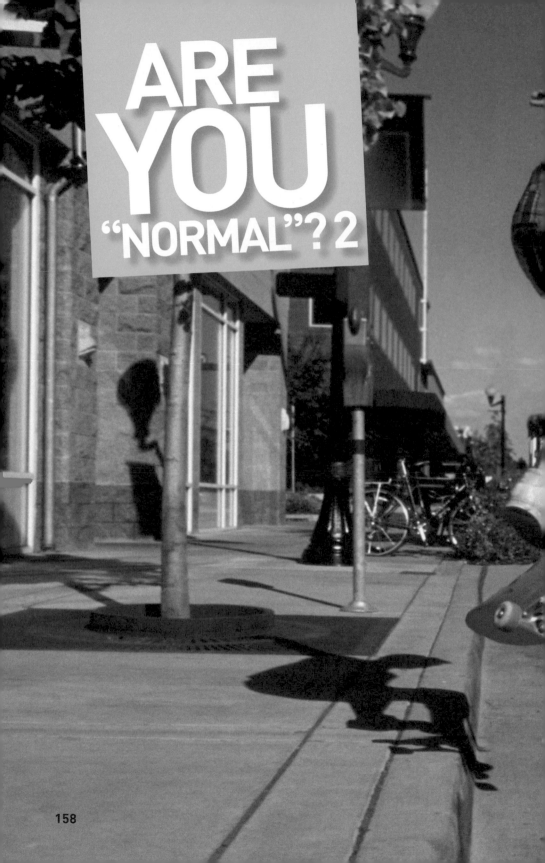

FUN

FUN QUiZ

BE SURE TO KEEP
TRACK OF YOUR
ANSWERS!

1 YOU'RE JAMES BOND AND YOU'RE IN TROUBLE! WHAT'S YOUR GET-AWAY VEHICLE GOING TO BE?

- Helicopter
- Glider
- Jet Ski
- Car
- Plane
- Bus
- Submarine
- Snowmobile
- Boat
- Train
- Taxi

2 HAVE YOU EVER WON A TROPHY?

- Yes
- No, but I want to
- No, and I'm not interested

3 IF YOU COULD MEET ANYONE, REAL OR FAKE (OR BOTH!), WHO WOULD IT BE?

- Fictional character
- Singer
- Famous actor/actress
- Sports superstar
- Political figure
- Other

4 IT'S MALL DAY! WHERE DO YOU WANT TO GO FIRST?

- Clothes store
- Pet store
- Toy store
- Tech store
- Game center
- Food court
- Just hang out by the fountain
- I don't want to go!

160

5 WHAT'S YOUR FAVORITE WILD ANIMAL?

- Tiger
- Elephant
- Giraffe
- Crocodile
- Koala
- Seal
- Wolf
- Dolphin
- Panda
- Penguin
- Snake
- Spider
- None of the above

6 WHAT'S YOUR FAVORITE THING TO DO AT THE PARK?

- Hang out
- Playground
- Play with a dog
- Organized sports
- Run
- Picnic
- Walk
- Toss something around
- Something else

7 WHAT'S YOUR FAVORITE THING TO WRITE WITH?

- A pencil
- A pen
- A marker
- A paintbrush
- A finger in something messy
- A computer
- Something else

8 WHICH "S" JOB WOULD YOU LIKE BEST?

- Spy
- Scientist
- Singer
- Star
- Storm-chaser
- Surfer
- Skateboarder
- Superhero

9 WHAT'S YOUR #1 SOURCE FOR MUSIC?

- Computer
- MP3 player
- Radio
- Home stereo
- Friends
- I make my own.

161

1

GET OUT OF THERE!

You're James Bond and you're in trouble! What's your get-away vehicle going to be?

HERE'S HOW KIDS SPLIT THE WAY THEY'D SPLIT:

20% want a helicopter to lift them away, chop-chop.

15% think glider soaring would be less boring.

14% say a Jet Ski would leave the bad guys in their wake.

13% would use a car. Because you know how cool that car would be.

12% say they'd take wing. And tail. And airplane jet engine.

11% voted for a sub—after they get inside, of course.

6% would want a snowmobile to hurry in a flurry.

3% think boats are best. And we're not talking rowboats.

2% would hop on a train. Ideally, from the top of a cliff.

2% would tell the cab driver, "Take me to my hideout!"

And 1% would hop on a bus. Hopefully, not a crowded bus.

WEIRD-O-METER HELICOPTER/GLIDER/JET SKI/CAR/AIRPLANE/SUB = 2, SNOWMOBILE = 3, ALL OTHER ANSWERS = 4

2 GOLD? SILVER? BRONZE? PLASTIC?

EVER WON A TROPHY?

➤ **1 IN 4 KIDS (26%) haven't won a trophy. But just you wait!**

➤ **1 IN 12 KIDS (8%) haven't won one and didn't want one.**

➤ **And the winner is . . . trophy winners. 2 OUT OF 3 KIDS (66%) say they've been victorious. And they can prove it.**

WEIRD-**O**-METER YES = 2, NOT YET = 3, I DON'T WANT ONE = 4

3 WHO IN THE WORLD?

IF YOU COULD MEET ANYONE, REAL OR FAKE (OR BOTH), WHO WOULD IT BE?

Somebody fake is the real winner. 1 in 4 kids (25%) want to meet a fictional character.

1 in 5 (20%) want to get in tune with a famous singer, maybe even on stage.

Another 1 in 5 (19%) would rather act naturally with an actor or actress.

1 in 10 kids (10%) hope to come off the sidelines and hang with a sports star.

Just 1 in 33 kids (3%) voted for a political figure. Go figure.

"NONE OF THE ABOVE" seems to be very popular. Nearly 1 in 4 kids (23%) desire to meet this mysterious person.

WEIRD-O-METER   FICTIONAL CHARACTER/SINGER/ACTOR/NOT LISTED = 2, SPORTS STAR = 3, POLITICAL FIGURE = 4

4 THE BUCK STARTS HERE!

IT'S MALL DAY! WHERE DO YOU WANT TO GO FIRST?

It's not even close—it's clothes! A stylish 30% of kids have a passion for fashion when they hit the stores.

Got puppy eyes for a pooch? Smitten with kittens? Just like the 21% who put pets first. Or maybe you just like the smell?

Tech store, toy store, and game center are all tied at 10%, 10%, and 10%. But really, when you think about it, is there so much difference between them?

Hungry kids (6%) know where to go: the food court.

And if you're the just-hang-out kind, you're not alone. In fact, 3% are sitting by the fountain with you.

Wait? What? You don't want to go to the mall? You're not that weird. 11% would rather drop than shop.

WEIRD-O-METER CLOTHING STORE/PET STORE = 2, TECH STORE/TOY STORE/GAME CENTER/DON'T LIKE THE MALL = 3, ALL OTHER ANSWERS = 4

165

5 GRRR? SNARL? HISS?

What's your favorite wild animal?
The answers could fill a year's worth of
National Geographic!

DOLPHIN 17%
WOLF 16%
TIGER 12%
PANDA 11%
PENGUIN 6%
SNAKE 6%
ELEPHANT 5%
KOALA 5%
GIRAFFE 4%
CROCODILE 3%
SPIDER 1%
SEAL 1%
NONE OF THE ABOVE 13%

WEIRD-O-METER DOLPHIN/WOLF/TIGER/PANDA = 2, PENGUIN /SNAKE/ELEPHANT/KOALA/GIRAFFE = 3, CROCODILE /SPIDER/SEAL = 4, NONE OF THE ABOVE = 2

6 A WALK IN THE PARK?

WHAT'S YOUR FAVORITE THING TO DO AT THE PARK?

- 23% give "hang out" the biggest shout-out.
- 18% spend the day on the playground.
- 15% play with a pooch.
- 7% team up for organized sports.
- 7% take their sneakers for a run.
- 5% pick packing a picnic.
- 4% wander and walk.
- 3% toss and catch a round, flat, or oblong object for fun.
- And 18% say, "None of the above." Hope it's fun.

WEIRD-O-METER HANG OUT/PLAYGROUND/DOG/SOMETHING NOT ON THIS LIST = 2, SPORTS/RUN = 3, ALL OTHER ANSWERS = 4

7 THE WRITE CHOICE?

WHAT'S YOUR FAVORITE THING TO WRITE WITH?

Pencils are the sharpest choice with 33%.

Computers are the right type for 25%.

A pen clicks with 23% of kids.

3% pointed to finger paints and other handy messes.

5% make markers their permanent choice.

4% bristle if they can't have a paintbrush.

?
And 7% say "something else," which could include quills, lasers, nails, and cake frosting tubes.

WEIRD-**O**-METER PENCIL/COMPUTER/PEN = 2, SOMETHING ELSE = 3, ALL OTHER ANSWERS = 4

8 SELECT SOME SPECTACULAR SPECIALTY!

Which "S" job would you like best?

- Stealthy, Secret Spy: 25%
- Smart, Sophisticated Scientist: 24%
- Spectacular, Silver-tongued Singer: 21%
- Sizzling Star of Stage and Screen: 12%
- Strong, Solid Superhero: 7%
- Scare-seeking Storm-chaser: 4%
- Slick, Smooth Surfer: 4%
- Seriously Sweet Skateboarder: 3%

WEIRD-O-METER SPY/SCIENTIST/SINGER = 2, MOVIE STAR/SUPERHERO = 3, ALL OTHER ANSWERS = 4

9 IS IT MUSIC TO YOUR EARS?

WHAT'S YOUR #1 SOURCE FOR MUSIC?

29%

Nearly 1 in 3 kids get their music from MC PC, DJ Mac, or another kind of computer.

13%

About 1 in 8 kids prefer the sound of their own music.

24%

Another 1 in 4 would rather tune in to the radio.

4%

1 in 25 prefer the big speakers on their home stereo.

26%

MP3 players play the hits for more than 1 in 4 kids.

4%

And the rest say their friends are their main source of tunes. Because that's what friends are for.

WEIRD-O-METER COMPUTER/RADIO/MP3 PLAYER = 2, KARA-OKE = 3, ALL OTHER ANSWERS = 4

WHERE ARE YOU ON THE WEIRD-O-METER?

ADD UP YOUR SCORE AND YOU'LL GET A WEIRDNESS NUMBER THAT'S MORE FUN THAN A BARREL OF MONKEYS.

1–23

YOU'RE AS NORMAL AS RIDING A BIKE.
Your ideas of fun may be predictable, but they hopefully won't threaten your life. There are so many great ways to spend time, and you've got some tried-and-true choices that don't let you down. Your favorite stores: clothes and pets (but not clothes for pets). Your favorite "S" job: spy. No matter where you go, you're always bringing the fun with you. And, perhaps, some bandages for when your less-normal friends have their fun.

YOU'RE AS NORMAL AS RIDING A HORSE.

Looking for fun? Chances are you're a fun-seeking missile. You don't pick the safest bets, or make the easiest choices, right? Why turn on music when you can start a band? Why pick an "S" job when you can choose one that starts with "Z"? Your spare time is a ripe time for making a splash. And whatever job you end up with, it won't be a dull one. Your taste for fun is so out there, you'd probably bond with Bond. James Bond.

YOU'RE AS NORMAL AS RIDING A UNICORN.

You like to hang with friends and would like to hang glide too. And you would rather surf than bike. Even on cement! Now that you know you're not normal about fun, stand tall! You make choices that others don't. (Or are afraid to.) Mavericks like you bring interesting fun . . . and wild horses couldn't drag you to make the boring choices. Drills bore. You rock.

BEHIND THE POLLS

So, just how did we go about collecting the opinions of kids like you? Simple—we put the polls online! We posted each question to the National Geographic Kids' website and got the truth straight from the source, our readers. Over the course of several months, we received thousands of answers to our zany questions until we had enough answers to get an idea of the thoughts and opinions of kids just like you. To discover what was normal, we took the average of those results to come up with our calculations. So while the opinions reflected in this book are not scientific fact, we hope you thought they were a lot of fun!

For more polls, quizzes, games, photos, facts, and fun, visit us online at kids.nationalgeographic.com.

Hope to see you again soon!

DEDICATED TO SOME ABNORMALLY FANTASTIC MOMS:
KARA, ESTHER, BARBARA, ANNA, KIM, MARTHA, NANCY, RACHEL, SUSIE, & SUZIE

AND IF YOU LIKE ANAGRAMS AS MUCH AS I DO . . .
The National Geographic Society
genial, earthy, iconic photos.

Now find the matching letters in each incredible NG teammate:

Rebecca Baines = ace brains

Eva Absher = she brave, A+

Kathryn Robbins = by ink arts born

Lori Epstein = list pioneer

Jennifer Emmett = refinement

Nancy Feresten = serene, canny

Melina Bellows = same noble will

Anne McCormack = nice mac monk

Without these weirdly wonderful women, you wouldn't be holding this fun book in your hands.

Thanks for reading!

—**Mark Shulman**